THE TRUTH ABOUT
Economics

THE TRUTH ABOUT
Economics

A CRITICAL THINKING GUIDE FOR
Students, Parents, Teachers and Citizens

MICHAEL RYAN

Columbus, Ohio

The Truth about Economics: A critical thinking guide for
Students, Parents, Teachers and Citizens

Published by Gatekeeper Press
3971 Hoover Rd. Suite 77
Columbus, OH 43123-2839
www.GatekeeperPress.com

ISBN: 9781619848337
eISBN: 9781619848320

Printed in the United States of America

This book is dedicated to the industrious students, young or old, who want to know how economic systems truly work.

This book is dedicated to the parents who want their children to learn how to prosper in our demanding and fast changing economic community.

This book is dedicated to those who will join the effort to change our educational system to ensure our children are taught relevant and meaningful economic concepts commonly referred to as financial literacy.

CONTENTS

INTRODUCTION

How This Book Came About

NEVER IN MY life did I expect to write a book. My initial career path had nothing to do with writing books. Instead, my early career was analytical, finding ways to use technology to solve business problems. My formal training included engineering and finance, with degrees from Texas A&M University and University of California Berkeley. This formal training enabled me to conceptualize and build bridges between technology and economics, making businesses more profitable. It was a rewarding career that allowed me to retire early and pursue avenues to give back to the community. One such avenue was teaching high school as a second career. Most classes I taught were related to mathematics, except for one random assignment to teach an economics class. Once I stumbled across the pervasive faulty logic that serves as the foundation of economics as taught today, I had to expose it.

As a teacher, I have always needed to explore the material at an exhaustive level in order to properly convey my understanding to a classroom of students with varying degrees of interest and capabilities. One explanation might work for one group of students, while a second might be required for a different group of students. This approach was fostered by my engineering training and is rooted in my innate curiosity about how things work. In the past, my curiosity has driven me to take things apart that probably should have stayed together. The carburetor in my 69 Chevy is a great example of something better left alone.

I approached the curriculum as I had approached the carburetor. The curriculum was disassembled and explored far beyond the intentions of the original manufacturer. To help with the exploration, I joined the online AP Economics Teacher Community as a source for further clarification. Soon, I found economic laws that conflicted with basic rational thought. My engineering mind just kept asking questions, digging deeper and deeper. My technology training demanded the resolution of why, why, why? The explanations from the AP community resources were fraught with circular logic.

At one point, I was told I didn't understand the math. "Them's fighting words". Any self-respecting engineer would not take such a comment lying down. The result is this book, which provides a complete exposure of how and why the theories involving supply and demand curves, originally conceived long ago, are incorrect and inadequate for explaining anything related to modern economics. At best, the theories are academic wall paper, created years ago as universities sparred for the Crown of Economics within Academia. The theories are now faded and torn, irrelevant, and mysteriously kept in place for some obscure purpose.

This book takes a structured rational approach to explaining the errors of old economic theories and their irrelevance to the economy of today. Readers with the patience and willingness to think critically will be greatly rewarded. They will learn why the old theories should be discarded. They will learn that there are several types of markets, including product markets, labor markets, and security markets. They will learn the six factors that affect the market for products, and the subsequent price one must pay. Later books in the series will delve into factors affecting labor and security markets.

Some of the concepts covered may be unfamiliar to many people. However, everyone can benefit from reading this book. The difference between financial literacy and the out of date economics curriculum is something everyone should understand. Anyone who is taking an economics class, or has a student or friend in an economics class, will discover a treasure of discussions this book creates, revealing financial literacy as the knowledge they need.

During my research, I was often told that economists do not use supply and demand curves in real life. When asked why the topics are still taught, the answer was that students would encounter the material and needed to be familiar with the concepts. The problem with this approach is that the students are never told that supply and demand curves fail to reflect reality. Instead, they are left with the impression that supply and demand curves represent the founding principles of economic science.

A relevant quote:

"This is what economics now does, it tells the young and susceptible (and also the old and vulnerable) that economic life has no content of power or politics because the firm is safely subordinate to the market and the state, and for this reason it is safely at the command of the consumer and citizen. Such an economics is not neutral. It is the influential and invaluable ally of those whose exercise of power depends upon an acquiescent public." John Kenneth Galbraith (1973)

People often say the system is rigged. Few understand that it starts with our own educational system, shaped and crafted by academia to develop an acquiescent public. Paul Samuelson is beyond any doubt the leading crusader in promoting the ideology to the American public.

> "I don't care who writes a nation's laws, or crafts its advanced treaties, if I can write its economics textbooks." Paul Samuelson—Nobel Prize Winner Economics 1970

Future Generations Will Pay the Price

For the most part, we fail to educate our children about the basics of managing their finances. We fail to teach our children how to prosper. There are several states that have attempted to define a curriculum for financial literacy. Only four, Utah, Tennessee, Missouri and Virginia, have added financial literacy as a requirement for graduation from high school. This situation needs to change. The value to students of understanding credit, investing, leverage, risk, retirement planning/Social Security, and the other many topics presented in a financial literacy class far out-weighs any value associated with old economic theories based upon unproven and unseen curves.

Economics today teaches students what to think.

Financial literacy teaches students how to think.

We need to stop teaching hollow and out dated economic theories that leave students misinformed and unprepared.

Highlights by Chapter

Chapter 1: How We Gather Knowledge—A review of how society, through science, promotes a concept from idea to knowledge, plus some common pitfalls along the way.

Included is a warning about how certain pitfalls can be used to confuse and mislead, hiding true knowledge and leading to ideology.

Chapters 2 and 3: Supply Curve and Demand Curve—A discussion of logical flaws found in the economic laws of supply and demand.

Chapter 4: Market Pricing—An introduction to the six factors that affect the price consumers pay in a product market.

Chapter 5: Economic Card Tricks—Mathematical errors, better described as card tricks, used by economists to justify their theories. Any theory that uses false mathematics as a justification is not scientific, but ideological.

Chapter 6: Economic Smokescreens—How economists purposely hide key concepts, such as profits, thus avoiding any questions about an equitable society.

Chapter 7: Replacing Supply and Demand—With some help from early economists, a better way to view a market for products is revealed.

Chapter 8: Groupthink—How the psychology of groups prevented academia from applying the basic concepts of science to economics. Old theories were rationalized into mythical proportions, freezing any new thought.

Chapter 9: Lessons Better Learned—Financial literacy embodies the knowledge and skills our children must have in order to prosper in our economic world. This chapter reviews those skills, and demonstrates how state governments thwart our children's access to this vital knowledge.

Chapter 10: Improved Vision—Some examples of how financial literacy leads to a better understanding of economics.

CHAPTER 1

Obtaining Knowledge

"I'm not a scientist. I'm interested in protecting Kentucky's economy."

—Mitch McConnell,
Cincinnati Enquirer October 3rd, 2014

CONTRARY TO MITCH McConnell's claim, everyone is a scientist to some degree. Science is more than physics, chemistry, or biology. Science, in the broadest sense, is the pursuit of knowledge. The different specialties in science are fields of study. Humans are constantly in search of knowledge and understanding, and are often trapped when they use improper methods. The scientific process is nothing more than a set of procedures to help the human mind avoid common errors of logic as society progresses down the road to knowledge.

Francis Bacon

The seeds for the modern scientific process were first published by Francis Bacon in 1620. His seminal work, *Novum Organum*, describes the framework for scientific exploration and knowledge development. There are three key aspects from *Novum Organum* that everyone should understand.

- His identification of idols as sources of error in human understanding
- His rejection of syllogisms
- His stress of the importance of observation and experimentation

Bacon on Idols

Bacon identified four types of idols that are basically preconceived notions from four different sources that may prevent someone from properly understanding an observed phenomena.

- **Idols of the tribe:** This idol or risk is related to basic human inability to perceive something. An example would be the inability to see the moons of Jupiter without a telescope or the difficulty humans have in thinking beyond three dimensions.
- **Idols of the cave:** This idol is associated with the bias or preconceptions of a single person. "For everyone has a cave or den of his own, which refracts and discolors the light of nature, owing either to his own education, or to the authority of those whom he esteems and admires . . ."
- **Idols of the Marketplace:** This idol refers to how groups or specialists can create their own confusion. Today, this could be associated with what is called Groupthink, a powerful deterrent to finding proper understanding and true knowledge.

- **Idols of the Theater**: This idol is associated with learning improper ideas or applying ideas learned in one area improperly to another. Economists have referred to this idol by the name of Scientism.

Bacon's identification of these various idols is about identifying bias in our thought processes. Without clearing the mind of preconceived notions, regardless of their source, any observation made is subject to error.

Bacon's final warning dealt with the human mind seeing things that were not there at all:

> "The human understanding is of its own nature prone to suppose the existence of more order and regularity in the world than it finds."

With some research, it can be shown that economists are prisoners of their own idols. A famous economist, Joseph Schumpeter, published an article in 1949 titled "Science and Ideology". In the article, Schumpeter claimed pre-held ideologies do not affect the scientific process of economists. If they did, it would be improper:

1. ". . . in itself scientific performance does not require us to divest ourselves of our value judgement or renounce the calling of an advocate of some particular interest. . . . It spells indeed misconduct to bend either facts or inferences from facts in order to make them serve either an ideal or an interest."

He also admitted that ideology distorts economic theory, as economists are not immune to bias:

2. "There is little comfort in postulating, as has been done sometimes, the existence of detached minds that are immune to ideological bias and ex hypothesis able to overcome it."[1]

Schumpeter was keenly aware that the creeds of economists are idols that block the light of unbiased observation. Economists' ideologies are held so strongly that economists jump for any fragment of information that supports their strongly held beliefs. The following quote on truth is relevant:

"We swallow greedily any lie that flatters us, but we sip only little by little at a truth we find bitter". Denis Diderot

Even though Schumpeter acknowledged the problem, he and other economists failed to take steps to ensure true knowledge was found using basic scientific methods.

Bacon on Syllogisms

Syllogisms are simple applications of logic that can lead to incorrect interpretations. They are more likely used to fool someone than to prove something. Therefore, Bacon was strongly opposed to their use.

As an example, consider the following statements and conclusions:

Statement 1: All men are mortal

Statement 2: Socrates is a man

Conclusion: Socrates is mortal (True)

---

1   Joseph A. Schumpeter, "Science and Ideology", *The American Economic Review*, March 1949, pg 358

Statement 1: The sun rises in the east and sets in the west

Statement 2: When sitting on the porch and someone walks around my house, they appear on the left and disappear on the right

Conclusion: The sun revolves around the earth. (False)

Statement 1: When the price for strawberries goes down, a person will buy more

Statement 2: Clothes, cars, and strawberries are goods.

Conclusion: If the price of cars goes down, a person will buy more cars. (False)

In most cases, a consumer buys one item and has no need for a second item.

The Laffer curve is another example of a syllogism.

Statement 1: Wealthy actors, such as Ronald Reagan, stop working in July because taxes reach the marginal rate of 70%. If tax rates go down, wealthy actors will work more, and the government will collect more taxes.

Statement 2: Wealthy actors are workers.

Conclusion: Cutting taxes on all workers will increase tax revenue. (False)

The false logic is due to the fact that most workers cannot stop working in July and sit on the couch. Most workers are not taxed at the marginal rate of 70%, but closer to an average rate of 15%. Cutting taxes for most workers reduces total tax revenue. Trickle-down economics is a false syllogism.

Bacon on Observation, Experimentation, and the Scientific Method

Today, Bacon's ideas are reduced to four steps that constitute the scientific method:

1. Observation and description of a phenomenon or group of phenomena.

2. Formulation of a hypothesis to explain the phenomena. In physics, the hypothesis often takes the form of a causal mechanism or a mathematical relation.

3. Use of the hypothesis to predict the existence of other phenomena, or to predict quantitatively the results of new observations.

4. Performance of experimental tests by several independent scientists. Repeated confirmations results in the acceptance of a theory. Experiments that fail to support predictions result in rejection, which restarts the observation and hypothesis phase.

In simple terms, the pursuit of knowledge is a continuous cycle. The following is an example of an early scientific discovery.

Spontaneous Generation

An early belief in the Middle Ages concerning how maggots appeared on dead meat was called spontaneous generation. The theory of spontaneous generation stated that various life forms would sprout in certain situations. The foundation of the theory came from the use of syllogisms and the lack of close observation. For instance, it was once believed that snakes could be generated by horse hairs in water.

In 1668, Francisco Redi conducted experiments that proved the hypothesis that fly eggs deposited in dead meat caused the appearance of maggots. Even so, in 1745, John Needham conducted experiments using boiled water and a newly invented microscope to provide experimental evidence that spontaneous generation occurred at the microscopic level. Twenty years later, Lazzaro Spallanzini replicated Needham's experiments with better controls and once again refuted spontaneous generation.

The end result is that human knowledge is continually refined and improved by the application of the scientific method. If a person fails to understand the impact of idols and syllogisms, or fails to use the proper methods of experimentation for achieving valid results, they will not find true knowledge. (See figure 1)

The economics profession is stuck on supply and demand curves and refuses to find any other explanation for economic activity. Supply and demand curves are the subtle foundation for *laissez faire* policies proclaiming that free markets solve all problems. The theories surrounding supply and demand do not allow for experimentation. Therefore, they represent ideas, or more broadly; they are best described as ideology.

In Chapter 8, an article published by Stanley Wong in *The American Economic Review* in 1973, is reviewed. Dr. Wong clearly shows that methodologies used by economists do not

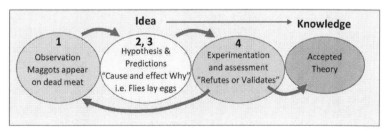

Ch 1 Figure 1

meet the standards of scientific methodology and are at best observations, with no predictive or explanatory value.

Economic Observations and Experimentation

Contrary to what economists tell us, it is fairly easy to confirm reality with observations. It is also possible to conduct thought experiments to test theories. Unfortunately, economists openly discourage the idea of exploring economic theories, with comments like the following:

> Mankiw 6th edition: "In economics, conducting experiments is often difficult and sometimes impossible.... Economists, like astronomers and evolutionary biologists, usually have to make do with whatever data the world happens to give them.

> Samuelson 1st edition: "We cannot perform the controlled experiments of the chemist or biologist. Like the astronomer, we must be content largely to "observe."

The authors achieve two objectives with these statements:

1. Associate their work with the legitimate work of other scientists

2. Dissuade any critical thinking with the idea that conducting experiments would be "difficult and sometimes impossible."

In reality, the laws and theories of economics fail to stand up to the simplest of experiments. Chapters 2 and 3 will show simple logic failures associated with supply and demand curves and will reveal the presence of fabricated data used to support the theories. Chapter 5 demonstrates planned deception using "mathemagics", or fake math, to create supply and demand curves that fail to conform to the basic rules of mathematics. These chapters are enough to prove obstruction of truth. Or as Schumpeter described:

> "It (advocacy) spells indeed misconduct to bend either facts or inferences from facts in order to make them serve either an ideal or an interest" [2]

The result is that economists are not scientists at all. They fail to follow the basic rules of observation and experimentation and, instead, use trite explanations about the difficulty of studying economics.

Rules of Good Scientific Practice

The importance of using honest scientific methods in the pursuit of any knowledge cannot be overstated. The importance is echoed by the Max Planck Society:

> – adopted by the senate of the Max Planck Society on November 24, 2000, amended on March 20, 2009 –

> "Scientific honesty and the observance of the principles of good scientific practice are essential in all scientific work which seeks to expand our knowledge and which is intended to earn respect from the public. The principles of good scientific practice can be violated in many ways— from a lack of care in the application of scientific methods or in documenting data, to serious scientific misconduct

---

2   Joseph Schumpeter, "Science and Ideology", *The American Economic Review*, March 1949 page 346

through deliberate falsification or deceit. All such violations are irreconcilable with the essence of science itself as a methodical, systematic process of research aimed at gaining knowledge based on verifiable results. Moreover, they destroy public trust in the reliability of scientific results and they destroy the trust of scientists among themselves, which is an important requirement for scientific work today where cooperation and division of labor are the norm."

CHAPTER 2

Supply Curve

"The purpose of studying economics is not to acquire a set of ready-made answers to economic questions, but to learn how to avoid being deceived by economists."

—Joan Robinson

THIS CHAPTER WILL demonstrate why there is no such thing as a supply curve and that the Law of Supply is not a law at all, but a deceptive tool to promote political policy. Five arguments are put forward.

1. Simple counter examples

2. Explanation of how a chart is not a function.

3. Clear evidence of fabricated data

4. Refutation of law of diminishing returns by a prominent economist

5. Groupthink response

Law of Supply

The Law of Supply states:

> "All else equal, an increase in price results in an increase
> in quantity supplied. In other words, there is a direct
> relationship between price and quantity: quantities
> respond in the same direction as price changes."

This great law of economics results in the equally famous
supply curve. Without the supply curve, many of the chart-
based theories of economics fall apart. Open your critical mind
while the foundations of this statement and the associated chart
are challenged. (See figure 1)

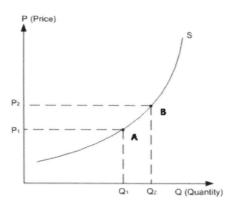

Ch 2 Figure 1 – Supply Curve

Art of Deception

This law has two parts—a distraction and a statement. The
distraction is the statement "all else equal". By phrasing the law
in this fashion, the student's mind is conditioned to accept the

second part of the statement without question. The reason is the structural phrasing follows what is referred to as a conditional statement. "IF A then B". There is no need to question B, as it only applies when A is encountered. The psychological effect is the mind accepts B to be true without challenge.

As a comparison, students that are familiar with conditional statements can confirm they do not represent laws. Consider a box of geometric shapes. (See figure 2) A conditional statement would be something like

"A polygon with three sides is a triangle."

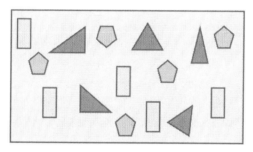

Ch 2 Figure 2 – Box of Shapes

The second statement—"Is a triangle" is not a law, it is an observation.

With the student's mind at rest, the law is delivered to their subconscious without challenge:

An increase in price results in an increase in quantity supplied.

This phrase may seem odd, but without the ability to challenge the instructor, the phrase is accepted as the indisputable truth.

But wait, what is a law? In science or math, a law is something that always applies and describes a phenomenon to the point of predicting outcomes. In physics, it could be Newton's laws relating force and acceleration, $F = MA$ or Einstein's $E = MC^2$. These laws always apply. Newton's second law does not say:

"Under the apple tree, Force is equal to mass times acceleration".

Newton's second law says $F = ma$. There are no preconditions.

This masquerade as a "law" provides tremendous cultural weight. Because the law came from a professor, a person of authority, the student deems the statement to be as solid as the laws of physics. The unsuspecting student has been duped.

An increase in price could scare buyers away, resulting in cuts in production or executives could lose their job for raising the price in the face of stiff competition.

The key to the trick is the pre-conditional statement, *all else equal*, sometimes referred to as *ceteris paribus*.

Dynamic Economy

There is no such thing as an economy frozen in time. Consider the dynamic nature of a body of water with waves, currents, and wind. Everything is in motion. (See figure 3) An economist studying the motion of the boat would propose the following law:

All else is equal, the boat will sail merrily along.

The wind never stays the same, the currents never stay the same and the waves never stay the same. Just as the conditions out on the deep blue sea always change, the conditions of human economic activity always change.

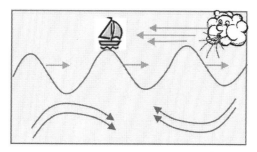

Ch 2 Figure 3 – Dynamic Environment

The economist has created an artificial world so far from reality it is of no value. However, with the students obediently following the lecture, they are unaware and unsuspecting. The law is delivered to the student's mind as a true fact.

An increase in price results in an increase in quantity supplied.

1. Counter Examples

With the law stripped of the confusing preconditions, students can recognize a method to explore the truth of the statement/ Law of Supply. The existence of one counter example will prove the law false.

An increase in price results in an increase in quantity supplied; inversely, a decrease in price will result in the quantity supplied to decrease.

Figuratively this could be represented as $(P\uparrow, Q\uparrow)$ *or* $(P\downarrow, Q\downarrow)$. Arrows point the same way! Any example that does not have arrows pointing in the same direction, would represent a counter example that disproves the law.

Several counter examples come to mind . . .

1. A merchant selling tickets to a sold-out concert:
    Price goes up while quantity stays the same
    ($P\uparrow$, Q *same*) (fails test)

2. A merchant has a surplus and must offer a discount:
    Price goes down, quantity goes up. ($P\downarrow$, $Q\uparrow$) (fails test)

3. A merchant profiting at a given price sells more at the same price to increase profits.
    Price stays the same while quantity goes up
    (P *same*, $Q\uparrow$) (fails test)

4. A merchant raising a price in a competitive market:
    Price goes up, but the quantity goes down.
    ($P\uparrow$, $Q\downarrow$) (fails test)

5. A merchant lowering his price in a competitive market:
    Price goes down while volume goes up. ($P\downarrow$, $Q\uparrow$) (fails test)

6. Inflation/Deflation:
    Price changes, but quantity stays the same
    ($P\uparrow\downarrow$, Q *same*) (fails test)

A favorite quote from Einstein –

"No amount of experimentation can prove me right, a single experiment can prove me wrong."

The law of supply is proven false.

"An increase in price <u>does not</u> always result in an increase in quantity"

A classical economist, at this point, claims the market sets the price, not the merchant. This is nonsense. Price is a negotiated item between a buyer and a seller. Both parties agree on price before any sale takes place. Consider the sold-out concert. The person holding a ticket sets the price they want to receive. They either sell the ticket or have to drop the price. There is no sure thing. If you examined the ticket sales for a sold-out concert, you will find quantity sold equals capacity, with a myriad of prices paid. There is not a single price that establishes equilibrium.

The market allows a price as high as someone will pay and as low as a merchant will sell. No single price is established. Markets do not enforce pricing at any level.

Double Check

Just to make sure nothing has been missed, the concept of "all else equal" can be re-applied. All else equal means everything but price and quantity provided are held constant. Economists would place the following items in the list of "all else held constant".

1. Income of buyers

2. Number of buyers

3. Price of other complementary/substitute products

4. Characteristics of products are the same. (all "Tickets" are the same, all automobiles are the same, all bushels of wheat are the same)

Even in using the famous stricture *ceteris paribus*, the Law of Supply does not stand. It is nothing more than conjecture that has been proven false.

From Motley Fool: The Fallacy of *Ceteris Paribus*

> "A *ceteris paribus* fallacy is based on an assumption that all else is equal in a particular analysis or will remain equal if a particular variable is changed. An 'all else is equal' reduction is sometimes a useful way to predict the impact of making a particular change, but in the real world, there are many times when it can't even assume a hint of a shade of a glimmer of validity."

Ceteris Paribus is unrealistic.

Purposeful Charade

Economics is not a science and should not pronounce laws as if it were a science. Pretending to be a science is just a way to bolster credibility and hide intent.

> "For far too long, economists have sought to define themselves in terms of their supposedly scientific methods. In fact, those methods rely on an immoderate use of mathematical models, which are frequently no more than an excuse for occupying the terrain and masking the vacuity of the content." Thomas Piketty

Economic text books clearly charade as a science. In Mankiw's 6th edition of his text book, Chapter 2 has a sub-section (page 22) titled "The Scientific Method: Observation, Theory, and more Observation". The book claims economists follow the cyclical challenge of observation and theory. This is not true. Chapter 5 of this book will provide solid evidence that observation is not practiced by economists. Later in this chapter, the presence of fabricated data in economic models is revealed. Scientists do not fabricate data, yet economic theories depend upon fabricated data. Mankiw's book goes on to explain how economists use assumptions in a similar way to physicists. From Mankiw . . .

"The assumption that gravity works in a vacuum is reasonable for studying a falling marble, but not for studying a falling beach ball."[3]

Mankiw's odd statement doesn't make any sense. Any student that has taken physics knows that gravity is not an assumption, but a physical phenomenon that affects the motion of all bodies, marbles and beach balls alike. Mankiw's statement confuses the student with the sole purpose of trying to sound like a scientist.

Paul Samuelson's original text book from 1948 was quick to grab the mantle of scientific method as well. On page 4, Samuelson boldly states . . . "It is the first task of modern economic science to describe, to analyze to explain, to correlate. . . ." Again, this is just part of the charade.

2. A Chart Is Not a Function Historical Beginnings of Supply Curve—Alfred Marshall, 1890

In Book V Chapter 2 *Principals of Economics*, Marshall introduces the concept of a supply schedule and a demand schedule. (See figure 4)

---

3   Gregory Mankiw, *Principles of Economics,*6th edition, South-Western Cengage Learning, 2008, page 23

Price	Quantity producers are willing to sell at given price	Quantity buyers are willing to buy at given price
37	300 Supplier Group X	600 Buyer Group C
36	100 Supplier Group Y	100 Buyer Group B
35	600 Supplier Group Z	200 Buyer Group A

Ch 2 Figure 4 – Marshall's Data

For a student taking a statistics class, analyzing this data falls into the study of categorical variables. Someone might present the supply information in one of the following ways: (See figure 5)

These charts are somewhat useful, but they do not present a supply curve that economist believe in today. Alfred Marshall took the liberty of creating a supply curve by organizing his suppliers from least expensive to most expensive and adding quantity produced to the bottom axis of his chart, creating the upward sloping supply curve. Or more bluntly, he made it up. (See figure 6)

However, the chart is just an illusion. It's an arbitrary

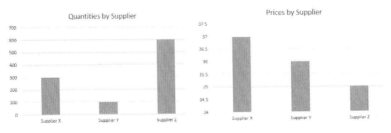

Ch 2 Figure 5 – How to display categorical data

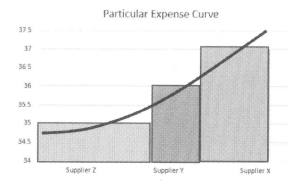

Ch 2 Figure 6 – How not to display categorical data

diagram showing production quantities and desired price in a convenient order. It provides the illusion that supplier Z sells his product first. It is entirely possible that supplier X harvested earlier in the year and sold his product to Buyer C, who was willing to pay $37.

Furthermore, Marshall adds the curved line and presents the data as a mathematical function with all the properties attributed to a true mathematical function. This is mathematical and scientific nonsense.

No mathematician would agree to this! Functions represented by curves require a fixed sequencing from left to right, based upon an input value (x). This is referred to as sequential dependence; functions must proceed from lower to higher values in sequence. In physics, this could be time. For the three suppliers x, y, and z, there is nothing that substantiates a fixed order from left to right. This is true for all categorical data. Unfortunately, Marshall was grasping for straws to support his theories, and no one corrected him.

Most high school math students will sense something is wrong. However, the instructor is granted respect and authority

by virtue of their position and the student is left puzzling about
the process. Some may scratch their heads and wonder:

> *"The things that pass for knowledge I can't understand"*
> *Steely Dan Reeling in the Years.*

Marshallian Function

As described earlier, a function has very precise rules. Consider
the distance function shown. (See figure 7) The rules for a
mathematical function are fairly simple.

1. The value of time is referred to as the independent
    variable. The value of time must proceed from left
    to right in a sequentially continuous manner.

2. The value of distance is related to the value of
    time and also moves in a sequentially continuous
    manner up or down.

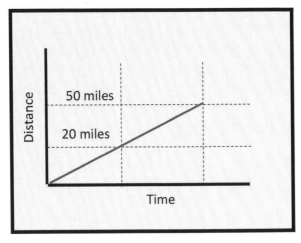

Ch 2 Figure 7 – The fish are getting bigger

The Marshallian function is false mathematics.

Consider a fishing tournament with twelve fishermen. Each fisherman catches one fish and returns to the marina for a weigh-in. The person running the tournament records the weight of each fish and places the data in a spreadsheet. Alfred Marshall would study the weights of the fish, arrange them from smallest to largest, and reach the conclusion that the more fish the tournament catches, the larger they will be. (See figure 8)

Marshall's function does not follow the rules noted above.

- His order from left to right is arbitrary. His order is based upon the conclusion Marshall is looking for—an upward sloping curve. He could just as easily reversed the order and declared that weight decreases as more fish are caught.

Marshall is using the appearance of science to disguise his theories as legitimate.

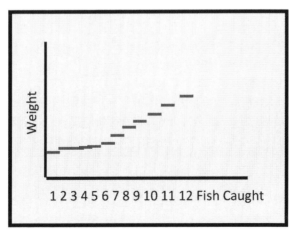

Ch 2 Figure 8 – The fish are getting bigger

This fallacy of casually using science was pointed out by a famous economist, Freidrich Hayeck, in "Scientism and the Study of Society," and agreed to by Schumpeter in his book "History of Economic Analysis". From Schumpeter's work:

"Scientism: This term has been introduced by Professor von Hayek to denote the uncritical copying of the methods of mathematical physics in the equally uncritical belief that these methods are of universal application and the peerless example for all scientific activity to follow. . . . As regards the question of principle, there cannot be the slightest doubt that Hayek is right . . . and so were all who in the nineteenth century preceded him in uttering protests similar to his—in holding that the borrowing by economists of any method on the sole ground that it has been successful somewhere else is inadmissible."[4]

Schumpeter claimed his work, *History of Economics* would clarify the situation:

"This history as a whole will answer the question whether there actually has been such uncritical copying"[5]

Schumpeter never addresses or answers his own question. The evidence is clear; not only were the methods copied, they

---

4   Joseph A. Schumpeter, History of Economic Analysis, Routledge, 1954 Page 15

5   Ibid page 15

were purposely distorted and misapplied to create economic theories for supply and demand curves.

Sadly, for society, the economics profession ignored Hayek's concerns.

Marshall's Fallacy

Alfred Marshall's conclusion from his table of data was a pair of supply and demand curves as shown with an equilibrium price of 36 and an equilibrium quantity of 700. (See figure 9)

However, this can't be equilibrium for two reasons:

1. Demand has not been fulfilled, as buyer A is still in the market for 200 bushels of corn

2. There is a surplus on the supply side, as supplier X has not sold his 300 bushels of corn.

Alfred continued glamorizing his theory with his concepts, like price elasticity. He defines elasticity using mathematical rules for the derivative or slope of a function. This adornment is mortar for the deception. The curves are not functions,

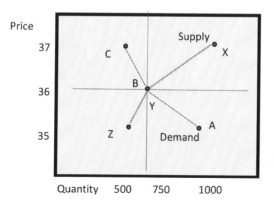

Ch 2 Figure 9 Supply and Demand?

but lines drawn across the top of categorical values. It is mathematically illegitimate to calculate the slope of a curve that improperly represents categorical variables. For the reader who is unfamiliar with these mathematical concepts, a short consultation with a strong high school math student will confirm these limitations.

The unsuspecting students are caught in a swamp of deception as they struggle to keep up with the unfamiliar ideas economists promote using misapplied mathematical concepts.

3. Fabricated Data

Law of Diminishing Returns (aka Increasing Marginal Cost)

Neoclassical Economics is founded on the premise of diminishing returns and the theory that diminishing returns causes increasing costs and an upward sloping supply curve. Students learn all about diminishing returns, diminishing marginal product, or diminishing marginal utility. Original economists were heavily influenced by the agriculture business, which is nothing like manufacturing. Unfortunately, economists ignored this difference and misapplied agricultural models to industrial age manufacturing economies.

Imagine a farmer with five hundred acres. When the farmer initiates his enterprise, he clears the land that has the most favorable soil conditions—perhaps, the land nearest the river. He finds this land very productive and achieves a high level of production on his first two hundred fifty acres. As he expands production, he clears land farther from the river, with perhaps less favorable soil conditions. The result is the yield per acre decreases and the cost per bushel of corn goes up.

This is predominantly what Alfred Marshall experienced.

He had limited exposure to modern production techniques or benefits of the industrial revolution. Henry Ford put an end to the law of diminishing returns with production processes that demonstrated constant or increasing returns. Other economists, such as Piero Sraffa, in his 1926 paper, "Laws of Returns", clamored for a more realistic view. Unfortunately, economists refused to abandon their theories that were dependent upon increasing costs, even though there was ample evidence to the contrary. Without increasing costs, the supply curve would be flat, and Alfred Marshall's supply and demand curves would be thrown out.

If someone were to prove there is no such thing as an upward-sloping supply curve, the theories based on supply and demand curves would fall apart.

Economics 101 Textbook and Marginal Cost

Examining the data from any Econ 101 text book will clearly show the data is fabricated. The following example comes from a Mankiw's 6th edition *Economics* textbook. (Mankiw page 266) Similar data can be found in college economics textbooks as well. The column for variable costs and associated marginal cost is completely fabricated and not seen in real life. (See figure 10)

When taking an economics class for the first time, the student is presented with the data above, and the student trusts that the instructor is telling the truth. However, by examining the variable cost column, it is easy to see that something is amiss. Why would the variable cost for the first two cups be 80 cents (40 cents per cup) and the variable cost for six cups be $4.80 (80 cents per cup). Why does variable cost go from 40 cents a cup to 80 cents a cup?

Quantity of coffee per hour	Total Cost	Fixed Cost	Variable Cost	Average Fixed Cost	Average Variable Cost	Average Total Cost	Marginal Cost
0	$ 3.00	$ 3.00	$ -				
1	$ 3.30	$ 3.00	$ 0.30	$ 3.00	$ 0.30	$ 3.30	$ 0.30
2	$ 3.80	$ 3.00	$ 0.80	$ 1.50	$ 0.40	$ 1.90	$ 0.50
3	$ 4.50	$ 3.00	$ 1.50	$ 1.00	$ 0.50	$ 1.50	$ 0.70
4	$ 5.40	$ 3.00	$ 2.40	$ 0.75	$ 0.60	$ 1.35	$ 0.90
5	$ 6.50	$ 3.00	$ 3.50	$ 0.60	$ 0.70	$ 1.30	$ 1.10
6	$ 7.80	$ 3.00	$ 4.80	$ 0.50	$ 0.80	$ 1.30	$ 1.30
7	$ 9.30	$ 3.00	$ 6.30	$ 0.43	$ 0.90	$ 1.33	$ 1.50
8	$ 11.00	$ 3.00	$ 8.00	$ 0.38	$ 1.00	$ 1.38	$ 1.70
9	$ 12.90	$ 3.00	$ 9.90	$ 0.33	$ 1.10	$ 1.43	$ 1.90
10	$ 15.00	$ 3.00	$ 12.00	$ 0.30	$ 1.20	$ 1.50	$ 2.10

Ch 2 Figure 10 – Mankiw's Data Fabrication

When looking closely at the variable cost/cup, and performing a regression, the following quadratic equation is found.

$$variable\ \frac{cost}{cup} = 0.1(\#\ of\ cups)^2 + 0.2(\#\ of\ cups) \qquad r = 1$$

This is the Scientism that Friedrich Hayek had warned about. Quadratic equations were taken directly from Isaac Newton's laws of motion and have no place in Economics.

$$Height = -9.8(time)^2 + Initial\ Velocity\ (time) + initial\ Height$$

With the help from a student in a statistics class, the meaning of $r = 1$ reveals that the data is a perfect fit for the equation. The economists did not make any observations of costs in a coffee shop; they made up the data to match the desired theory.

Why would the economist want the variable cost to follow exactly the square of quantity sold?

Answer: It is the only way the economist can create an increasing cost curve that becomes the basis for an upward-sloping supply curve. No one has ever actually found a real production process that has a variable cost function that follows a quadratic equation.

The data is completely fabricated. The students mind is being trained.

4. Refutation by a Leading Economist

Economists have resisted updating their models, even though prominent economists such as Piero Sraffa clearly showed a new approach was required. Economists were strongly motivated to ignore constant or decreasing marginal costs as these costs completely undermined their chart-based theories that use supply and demand curves.

Simply stated—recognizing the presence of constant or increasing returns and flat or downward sloping supply curves would require a re-write of all economic theories based upon supply and demand curves.

In Sraffa's own words from 1926 . . . "The Laws of Returns under Competitive Conditions" [6]

"there is one dark spot which disturbs the harmony of the whole. This is represented by the supply curve, . . . its foundations are so weak as to be unable to support the weight imposed upon them is a doubt which slumbers beneath the consciousness of many, but which most succeed in silently suppressing. From time to time someone is unable any longer to resist the pressure of his doubts and expresses them openly; then, in order to prevent the scandal spreading, he is promptly silenced . . ."

6   Piero Sraffa, "The Laws of Returns under Competitive Conditions", *The Economic Journal*, Blackwell, December 1926, pp 535-550

Much credit should be given to Piero Sraffa, who took risks to shake the establishment. Sraffa clearly pointed out that economics is not a science, but a method to train the mind. Challenges are rejected instead of inspected. It has been unfortunate that he did not shake hard enough and could not overcome the silent suppression of ideas.

5. Group Think Response—Suppression

The crazy part about this situation is that most economists knew they were stretching the boundaries of honesty. Consider this quote from Joseph Schumpeter's *History of Economics*. (1954 p. 41):

> "The role of what above is meant by conscious dishonesty is greatly enhanced by the fact that many things that do amount to tampering with the effects of logic do not in our field necessarily present themselves as dishonesty to the man who practices such tampering. He may be so fundamentally convinced of the truths of what he is standing for that he would rather die than give new weight to contradicting facts or pieces of analysis. The first thing a man will do for his ideals is lie."[7]

Here, Schumpeter admits that someone's ideology poses a risk to their honesty and the discovery of the truth. When someone is "so fundamentally convinced of the truths" that they would rather lie than admit their position/theories are incorrect, an ideology is born. This is exactly what Francis

---

7   Joseph A. Schumpeter, *History of Economic Analysis*, Routledge, 1954, page 41

Bacon warned of with regard to idols. This is an example of an "Idol of the Cave": a bias or preconception of an individual. When this idol is re-enforced with *groupthink pressures*, it is a significant impediment to finding the truth.

The groupthink response to Sraffa's opposing view was swift and complete. Schumpeter addresses Sraffa's paper on page 1012 in his book and references two articles by other economists, Viner and Young, which "clear up" the controversy. From Schumpeter's book:

"For instance, Professor Viner's famous paper on 'Cost Curves and Supply Curves' that, starting from Marshall's analysis, successfully cleared up a large part of the ground, appeared only in September 1931 (Zeitschrift für Nationalökonomie); Professor A.A. Young's paper on 'Increasing Returns and Economic Progress' only in December 1928 (*Economic Journal*)." [8]

If these works are examined closely, they are not very convincing. Viner's paper almost apologizes for the lack of rigor in the use of curves. Viner's second sentence reads:

"No attempt is made here at realistic descriptions of the actual types of relationships between cost and supply." [9]
Jacob Viner

Schumpeter claims Viner's paper cleared things up. The only

---

8   Ibid page 1012

9   Jacob Viner, "Cost curves and supply curves", *American Economic Association—Readings in Price Theory*, Allen and Unwin, 1953, pp 198-232

clarity is that supply and demand curves are not realistic, just as Sraffa claimed.

A.A. Young's paper is an impossible mountain of gibberish stretching to almost 7,000 words. However, if you peel back the 7,000 words of gibberish, you will find Young's honest assessment expressed in fewer than 40 words:

> "The apparatus which economists have built up for the analysis of supply and demand in their relations to prices does not seem to be particularly helpful for the purposes of an inquiry into these broader aspects of increasing returns." [10]

This sentence is buried in the middle of his 13-page document. Young agrees with Sraffa, but he buried his honesty. This is a form of self-censorship, one of the symptoms that is demonstrated by people that participate in groupthink. Groupthink will be covered in detail in Chapter 8.

This subterfuge happens all the time in economics. From an interview with James Kenneth Galbraith (6/1/2016):

> "Do economists self-censor any comments or research that challenges the status quo?

> "Self-censorship is part of the culture within which economists live. It is pervasive among those young enough to be on the cusp between free thought and professional obligations. Among economists who are a little bit older, fear of ridicule, ostracism, and quick rejection of papers

---

10   Allyn A. Young, "Increasing Returns and Economic Progress" , *The Economic Journal*, December 1928 page 533

is such that they arrive at a further stage, at which there is no need for self-censorship because critical thoughts do not occur to them in the first place."

Viner was participating in groupthink, and the group applauded him. His paper used Bacon's idols of the market-place by burying the discussion in magical words that only have meaning to economists. The language barrier prevents people from outside the profession from participating, requiring them to defer any understanding to economists. Even though Viner's paper clearly stated there was no "attempt at realistic description", later publications from economists hailed the paper as a success and declared that it "immediately changed the profession".[11]

Clearly the group had spoken and there would be no more discussion of declining cost curves or declining supply curves. The suppression was complete.

Ideology has been a major barrier to any realistic discussion of economic processes. From Steven Keen's Debunking Economics:

"Why is economics so resistant to change? Is it because everything economists believed at the end of the nineteenth century was correct? Hardly, as this book shows. Instead, to understand the incredible inertness of economics, we have to consider an essential difference between social sciences in general and the physical sciences, and the thorny topic of ideology."[12]

---

11   Thomas Cate Editor, *An Encyclopedia of Keynesian Economics*, 2nd Edition, Edward Elgar, 2013, page 668

12   Steve Keen, *Debunking Economics*, Zed Books, 2011 page 170

The economic theories related to supply and demand curves are equivalent to the Theory of Spontaneous Generation. They only persist to educate people into ignorance.

Conclusion

Economic theory using supply and demand curves is not realistic and should not be taught. The only things that can be learned from Neo-Classical Economics are how groupthink operates and how social engineering uses the education system to achieve certain goals.

CHAPTER 3

The Demand Curve

Existing economics is a theoretical system which floats in the air and which bears little relation to what happens in the real world.[13]

—Ronald Coase

THIS CHAPTER WILL disprove the Law of Demand and the associated demand curve. The arguments put forward comprise:

1. Counter examples

2. Common sense dismissal of the Personal Demand Curve

3. A more realistic view of demand

4. What they teach in business school

5. Beyond the bars

6. Concerns raised by economists that were ignored

7. Alfred Marshall admits limitations but nothing is done

---

13 An interview with Robert Coase 9.17.1997.. https://www.coase.org/coaseinterview.htm

Law of Demand

The Law of Demand states:

> "All else equal: an increase in the price of a good will result in the amount demanded to fall, and when the price of a good falls, the amount demanded rises."

Economists are so confident about this law that riches have been promised to anyone who can find a counter example.

> *"Assured of immortality, professionally speaking, and rapid promotion"* [14] George Stigler

Just as the law of supply has its famous supply curve, the law of demand has the equally familiar demand curve. (See figure 1)

Art of Deception

The reader will once again recognize the format of a conditional statement with the pre-condition of all else equal. Laws of science do not have pre-conditions. The formal structure of the conditional statement provides a false formality that relaxes the mind and allows a seemingly innocuous statement to enter your thoughts and find a permanent resting place.

> An increase in the price of a good will result in the amount demanded to fall, and when the price of a good falls, the amount demanded rises.

---

14   George Stigler, "Theory of Price", Macmillan, 1966, page 24

Ch 3 Figure 1

This statement sounds logically correct, so we accept the statement as true. The economist declares this as law and the student has little recourse other than to accept this law into their newly-trained mind.

1. Counter Examples

Recall that a law must always hold, even when Isaac Newton is not under the apple tree. Note that demand is from the purchaser's viewpoint, not the merchant, and any counter examples should be about the customer's response. There will be two ways to examine this law: how will a customer respond to a price increase, and how will a customer respond to a price decrease.

Satiation

It is surprising the idea of being full or satisfied is hardly mentioned in an economics text book. The books present a vague idea of marginal utility, described as when a person has more and more, they need less and less. Eventually, consumption stops. However, the satiation point in a text book is way beyond anything realistic.

Consider the following examples where a customer's needs have been met and no further purchases take place.

1. A customer only needs one item

2. A customer's needs have been met, and the customer can't store any items for future use.

3. A customer can't afford an additional item

Strike One—When a customer's needs have been met, or the consumer faces other constraints, dropping a price will not lead to an increase in the quantity purchased.

Timeframe

Consider the purchase of goods at the local department store. When prices are dropped for a sale, people flock to the store to buy more. But are they really buying more? If you consider the consumer's behavior for an entire year, you will see that the smart shopper is planning their purchase activity around the dates when products go on sale. Consumers are typically not buying more than they need unless they are infected by materialism or are committed hoarders. At some point, the closets are full and the shopping stops. It is more likely that a consumer will buy higher quantity of goods in one month and will abstain from purchasing those goods until they are again in need of something.

Strike Two—Dropping a price is a signal for buyers to come shop. Overall quantity is not increased. Placing an item on sale should be viewed as implicit negotiation for a better price.

Allocated Funds:

To the consumer, a good could be a generic car or a specific make and model for a car. When a consumer shops for a car, they typically have a budget in mind and will make a choice later about which car to buy. They shop for a period of time and finally make a selection. In the end, the consumer buys one car. Lowering the price will not induce that consumer to buy another car. Lowering the prices allows the consumer to buy a more expensive car at a discount or use unspent funds in another manner, such as savings.

Strike Three—Personal budgets constrain quantity demanded.

Similar Goods/Product Substitution

Consider the economists' favorite example—strawberries in season. Most people will in fact purchase more strawberries when they are in season, they taste great and the price has dropped. However, consumers are not buying more food. This is product substitution between similar goods. Instead of blackberries or some other fruit, the customer purchases strawberries. The fact that strawberries taste so much better in season is a factor ignored by economists.

Strike Four?—Dropping the price of a good that has substitutes will increase the sale of that one item relative to the substitutes, but will not increase the sale of that type of good.

Customer Must Have It—Monopoly, limited supply or protected product

Consider the situation where a customer is in a must have situation and the item they want to purchase is from a monopoly or has limited supply. In this situation, a price increase will not result in a decrease in quantity.

There can be many situations where a customer must have something from limited providers. Perhaps these are familiar:

1. A ticket to a sold-out concert—limited suppliers, limited quantity

2. The latest technology gadget or fad fashion, a protected product, i.e., patents or trademarks

3. Cancer-curing drugs—monopoly via patents

4. Food during war or famine–disrupted supply

In each of these situations, the quantity purchased is immune to price. The customer wants one ticket, one new cell phone, or one month of drugs to stay alive. The price he pays will depend upon his ability to negotiate and the seller's willingness to concede a price.

Economists are aware of this exception to the Law of Demand and provide a convenient caveat, referring to these goods as inelastic goods. The most common example of an inelastic good that economists use is gasoline. They clearly avoid the topic of high-priced pharmaceuticals or other goods that might raise the question of ethics or fairness. This reveals gasoline as a peculiar choice by economists, as consumers can change purchase decisions over time by deferring a trip. However, they cannot change their decision when it comes to life-saving medication. Economists are specifically avoiding any product discussions that might raise ethical questions.

You're "Out"—A merchant can raise the price, and quantity does not go down!

2. Common Sense Dismissal of the Personal Demand Curves

The typical textbook will introduce the personal demand curve as shown below from the Mankiw 6th edition textbook (page 68)[15] The book goes on to explain how the personal demand curve is combined/summed with other consumers to create the downward sloping market demand curve. (see figure 2)

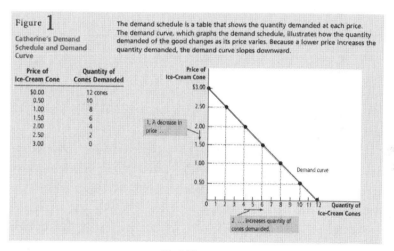

Ch 3 Figure 2

The unsuspecting student is told this is how people behave. The truth is the data is made up to support the Law of Demand

---

15 Gregory Mankiw, *Principles of Economics*, 6th edition, Cengage Learning, 2012, page 68

Catherines Demand Schedule		
Quantity of Cones	Price for Cones	Total Spend
1	$ 2.75	$ 2.75
2	$ 2.50	$ 5.00
3	$ 2.25	$ 6.75
4	$ 2.00	$ 8.00
5	$ 1.75	$ 8.75
6	$ 1.50	$ 9.00
7	$ 1.25	$ 8.75
8	$ 1.00	$ 8.00
9	$ 0.75	$ 6.75
10	$ 0.50	$ 5.00

A (rows 1–5)
B (rows 6–10)

Ch 3 Figure 3

and the companion downward sloping demand curve. No actual observations or thought experiments were provided to support this data. The student's ignorance is cemented with data and graphs that are crafted specifically to justify the Law of Demand.

The scientific method requires that observations happen first, followed by conjecture on possible cause and effect scenarios. The economics profession works in reverse—write a law and then create the data to support the law.

Catherine, is a consumer who is buying either 10 cones a month at 50 cents a cone or 1 cone a month at $2.75 a cone. (See figure 3). The fallacy Catherine's demand schedule becomes obvious when you consider the effect on Catherine's monthly budget.

A. Why would a consumer spending $2.75 a month for one cone suddenly spend $9.00 a month for 6 cones just because the price per cone drops to $1.50? Why wouldn't that consumer spend the $1.25 savings on something else?

B. Why would a consumer, who is paying 50 cents a cone for 10 cones and a budget of $5, suddenly be willing to spend $9, almost doubling her budget to obtain 40% fewer cones that have tripled in price? The economist ignores his own concoction of all else equal. Wouldn't the consumer have to re-allocate spending to accommodate the change and thus violate the all else equal condition?

Answer—this behavior has never been observed in real life. The economist is making up the data to support the model.

Consider the personal demand curve for most consumer purchases, i.e., Car, appliance, other. Consumers do not purchase more cars, appliances, baseball gloves, etc., when prices go down. (See figure 4)

Economists are using a syllogism to confuse people.

Statement 1: When strawberries go on sale, people buy more strawberries.

Statement 2: Strawberries and cars are products.

Conclusion: If the price of a car (or any product) goes down, people will buy more.

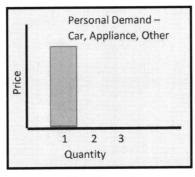

Ch 3 Figure 4

The law of demand and the demand curve are pure fabrications, based upon faulty logic using syllogisms.

3. A more realistic view of Demand

It is time to pause and think about what really happens with an individual's demand for an ice cream cone. First, time needs to be considered. Second, what is the person willing to pay? Third, what do they need? With these three simple thoughts, a more realistic view of personal demand can be found.

Each of the vertical lines represent a single purchase of an ice cream cone for a certain price. (See figure 5) Key attributes of a person's demand are:

1. The price a person will pay is completely dependent upon the person's perception of the market price range for an ice cream cone, their level of available income/budget, and the urgency of the need.

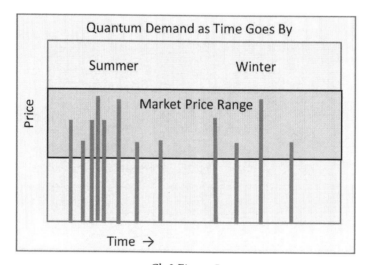

Ch 3 Figure 5

2. Quantity depends upon time or season, not price. Once a person is satiated, time must pass before they are willing to purchase an additional ice cream cone.

3. Purchases are not fluid. People do not purchase a cone after a set period of time has passed and they cannot purchase fractional increments. Purchases are quantum and random. A student in statistics will recognize that prices follow a distribution of some sort. They will also recognize that the time between purchases follows a distribution as well.

Item number one is very important as it clearly identifies the coupling that actually occurs between supply and demand. A person is aware of supply, given their familiarity with prices. It is tempting to dwell on the chicken and egg question–which came first, the ice cream cone supply or the ice cream cone demand? It doesn't matter which came first, but it does matter that the two exhibit an interdependent relationship that moves in the same direction for sustainable markets.

An individual's quantity demanded is not significantly affected by price, but primarily driven by need. This demand can be somewhat random in nature, as one day an ice cream cone will satisfy the need, while on other days a candy bar may satisfy the need. Economists mistakenly assume perfect information about pricing, allowing a consumer to make a split-second decision between a candy bar and an ice cream cone. This behavior doesn't happen in real life. The economist is focused on assumptions. A scientist would be focused on observations.

The concept of a quantum purchase is tricky, but critical for an improved understanding. Think of the consumer decision in terms of an on or off switch. A person either buys the product or does not buy the product. As long as the price is in the acceptable range, the purchase will take place when the need arises and funds are available. A marketing class may introduce the topic of Weber's Law, which states that small price changes are often overlooked by consumers, but larger price changes will cause the buyer to pause and re-consider the purchase. With a moderate price increase, a consumer may still buy, as the new price is not entirely outside an acceptable range or they don't have time to walk to the next ice cream stand for a possible lower price, but a future transaction with this vendor could be placed in jeopardy. This concept is best understood as Consumer Price Response. A single consumer will only change the purchase decision once a price has increased beyond their personal threshold. Considering that the decision to buy is affected by several factors, it is more apparent why the purchase appears as a random event to the seller.

Weber's Law is completely counter to Neoclassical Economics, which believes even small changes in price will result in a change in quantity consumed by the market.

When examining how a market will behave, all the buyers in the market need to be considered. Each buyer will have a different sensitivity to price changes. If a single provider raises their price, as the percentage of change increases, more and more customers "turn off" their purchase decision. The sales for this provider will eventually be reduced, but there is not a demand curve that can be used to predict consumer behavior.

If all providers raise their price, this behavior will happen over a period of time, and consumers gradually adjust their acceptable market price range. This is inflation, regardless of the cause. The customer will not likely change buying behavior because of smaller percentage changes. For larger price changes, they may reduce consumption of that good if they are constrained by wages that have not kept pace with inflation.

4. What They Teach in Business School

With the understanding that a purchase is an individual random event, the need to add individual demand curves to form a complete market demand curve goes away. This concept allows a business to treat demand as a quantity that is consumed in a market. This is exactly what is taught in business school. An excerpt from a textbook on marketing follows: *Principles of Marketing*—Prentice Hall.[16]

> ESTIMATING TOTAL MARKET DEMAND The total market demand for a product or service is the total volume that would be bought by a defined consumer group in a defined geographic area in a defined time period in a defined marketing environment under a defined level and mix of industry marketing effort. Total market demand is not a fixed number, but a function of the stated conditions. For example, next year's total market demand for ice cream in Canada will depend on how much the makers of Sealtest, Haagen-Dazs, Parlour, President's Choice, and other brands spend on marketing. It will also depend on many environmental factors, ranging from the level of consumer health concerns to the weather in key market areas.

Notice that price is not a factor for determining the size of the market. The business executive will then use breakeven

---

16   Philip Kotler, *Principles of Marketing* Prentice Hall

analysis and product mark up to determine a price that fits in the existing market price range. Sales targets are then set to achieve a target level of profit.

Why would academia teach business executives one thing while they teach the rest of America something else? Perhaps it is time to ask your State Board of Education or your child's University the same question.

An economist will tell you the business person is wrong and isn't thinking like an economist! A snippet from *Forbes by* June 15th 2012, by Peter Fader:[17]

> "Economists are an interesting breed. They have their heads in the clouds, dreaming of a magical world where people are rational, markets operate efficiently, and all kinds of other strict rules apply about what's right and wrong. In their vivid imaginations, they see upward-sloping supply curves, downward-sloping demand curves, and all the implications that arise from these and other assumptions. They're not particularly troubled by facts, often because the actual "rubber meets the road" data that would support or refute such assumptions are hard to find—especially when they're too busy balancing their delicate curves in a manner that often seems to defy the laws of physics."

There is absolutely no value in teaching people false concepts, unless there is an ulterior motive.

---

17 Peter Fader, Marketing vs. Economics: Gymnastics or High-Wire Act?, Forbes June 15th 2012

5. Beyond the Bars

If someone were to look beyond the bars of economic theory, a better picture of what a total market actually looks like would appear. Consider the auto market, with different types of consumers.

1. High-end luxury buyers (wealthy)
2. Affordable prestige buyers
3. Value buyers
4. Economy buyers

If we were to arrange these groups in descending price order the market would look like a downward sloping curve. (See figure 6)

This is the shape most people are thinking about when they picture a demand curve for auto's. This is why students are so easily fooled into believing there is a demand curve.

It is very important to understand that this is just a

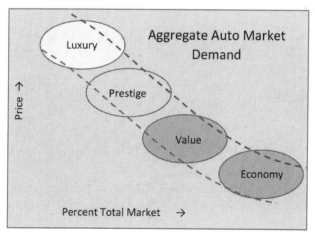

Ch 3 Figure 6

representation of a market. There is not a functional relationship between quantity and price. This is not a demand curve as taught by economics. Your statistics student will recognize this as a ranked cumulative frequency chart, sometimes referred to as an ogive!

Aggregate Supply for Cars

Describing the same market with a focus on suppliers would result in the Aggregate Auto Market Supply. (See figure 7)

1. Mercedes, Cadillac,

2. Lexus 460, Chrysler 500,

3. Ford, Chevy,

4. Fiesta, Civic, Corolla

Without the constraints of previous misconceptions, it can be seen that supply and demand are actually one and the

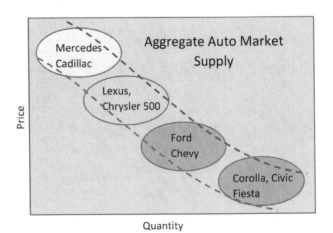

Ch 3 Figure 7

same. Supply and demand are not forces that push in opposite directions to determine price. Supply and Demand are two sides of the same transaction. Without a sale, there is no price.

6. Concerns Raised but Ignored

In the early 1900s, there were opposing views to Alfred Marshall's theories involving static equilibrium. H. L Moore wrote several works, including *Laws of Wages*, *Economic Cycles* and *Synthetic Economics*. Moore believed that static equilibrium was terribly flawed.

> "The assumptions underlying Marshals derivation of his law of demand are neither satisfactory nor indeed admissible."[18]

Alfred Marshall responded to the criticism by refusing to read Moore's works and refusing to meet with him. In a letter from Marshall to Moore . . . [19]

> "I will be frank. I have had your book on Laws of Wages in a prominent place near my writing chair ever since it arrived, intending to read it when opportunity came. It has not come & I fear it never will come. For what dips I have made into the book make me believe that it proceeds on lines which I deliberately decided not to follow many years ago . . . (Marshall to Moore, 5/6/1912 [1013])"

---

18   Henry Schultz, "The Chicago Tradition in Economics Volume 5" Published by Routledge 2002. Edited by Ross Emmett Page 125

19   David Teira Serrano, A Positivist Tradition in Early Demand Theory http://www2.uned.es/personal/dteira/docs/positivisttradition.pdf

H. L. Moore believed that statistical analysis should be used to substantiate economic theory and his works reported the finding of an upward sloping demand curve for pig iron. Economists that believed in Marshall's view of economics responded with critical articles. E. J. Working published an article "What do Statistical Demand Curves show?"[20]

"In the case of pig iron, however, professor H.L Moore finds a "Law of Demand" which is not in accord with Marshall's universal rule. He finds that the greater quantity of pig iron sold the higher the price"

Working tries to explain away the concern, starting with a description of Moore's statistical process as applied to the price of beef. He first plots "points." (See figure 8)

"First, we find out how many pounds of beef were sold in a given month and what was the average price. We do the same for all the other months in the period over which our study is to extend and plot our data with quantities as abscises (horizontal axis) and corresponding prices as ordinates. (vertical axis) Next we draw a curve to fit the points. This is our demand curve. "

Before drawing the curve, asking one question shows the folly. Do the points of interest represent the demand for a product tied to a purchase or do they represent the supply of a product as related to a sale? The answer is both. Once

---

20   E. J. Working, "What do statistical demand curves show?", *Quarterly Journal of Economics* Oxford University Press February 1927 volume 41 issue 2 pages 212-235

Price

Ch 3 Figure 8

again, supply and demand are shown to be two sides of the same coin.

Instead of recognizing a discovery that indicates there may be fundamental problems with the theory of market equilibrium with separate supply and demand curves, Working tries to rationalize the finding in a manner that is consistent with the original theory. At one point he promotes peculiar method for seeing what he wants to see. (See figure 9)

In Working's own words:

"It is altogether possible that shifts of the demand curve . . . be accompanied by shifts in the supply curve . . . and vice versa."

The result is the D' demand curve shown. Notice Working has ignored the cloud of points and selected only six points that would be consistent with old theories. Working has ignored Moore's observations.

Leontief was another economist that argued against H L Moore's findings. His logic suffered from the same arbitrariness of Working.

Michael Ryan

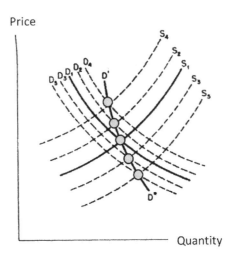

Ch 3 Figure 9

"Leontief looks at a scatter diagram of prices and quantities and sees in it traces of unrelated arbitrary shifting of hypothetical demand and supply curves.[21]

Setting aside preconceived notions, the observation confirms that a separate supply and demand curve have never been found. The second observation is that quantity and price change all the time. Given these are true, there is no such thing as static equilibrium. Holding fast to the static equilibrium model would be the same as if Isaac Newton one day saw objects fall as predicted but other days would observe objects floating into the skies, and still claim the law of gravity was universal. Without supporting observations, the theory of static equilibrium fails to explain reality.

---

21   Ibid Henry Schultz, Chicago Tradition . . . . page 129

Consider a scientist who observes a shadow of an object on the ground. The shadow is a perfect circle. One scientist from planet flat, who lives in two dimensions, proposes a theory that says the object casting the shadow is a round plate. A second scientist from a three dimensional planet proposes a theory that the object is an orb. A third scientist declares that both could be correct, but without more information you can't rule out the object is not the shape of a football.

The economist clinging to static equilibrium is effectively living on planet flat and is unable to see the truth of a multidimensional world. The economists, by virtue of their favorite distraction, *ceteris paribus/static equilibrium*—have confined themselves to blindness. Groupthink has closed the trap.

Professor Henry Moore knew something was incorrect and raised the following concern . . .

"The Doctrine of the uniformity of the demand function is an idol of the static state-the method of ceteris paribus-which has stood in the way of successful treatment of dynamic_problems." [22]

Moore understood the scientific process, however his quiet personality could not overcome Marshall's obstinacy. Coupled with the pressure of groupthink, Moore and the academic community were unable to discard a theory that fails to describe reality.

In a true scientific field, Moore's concerns would have been examined further. In the field of economics, it was ignored, just as Piero Sraffa's concerns about marginal cost were buried.

---

22   H. L. Moore, *Economic Cycles,* Macmillan, 1914, pg 64

7. Marshall Admits Limitations but Nothing Changes

To conclude, even Marshall admitted that *ceteris paribus* is problematic. In a letter from Marshall to Moore dated 1/16/1912 (Cited—*Probability Economics and Truth* by Hugo Kenzenkamp page 129) Marshall noted:

> "The ceteris paribus clause, though formally adequate seems to me impractible"

If *ceteris paribus* is impractible to Alfred Marshall, why is it at the core of a required class on economics? Why would someone want so badly to teach a false theory? Chapter 8 will examine the psychological pressure of group think.

8. Final Straw for Demand Curve

The demand curve is based upon utility theory, which imagines that people robotically respond to price decreases by purchasing more product, regardless of other demands that life places on them. Utility theory has since been disproven. In 2002, the Nobel Prize in Economics was awarded to Danny Kahneman for his work with Amos Tversky on prospect theory, which showed people do not rationally respond to inputs, as required in utility theory.

> *"Somehow, the economists felt that we are right and at the same time they wished we weren't because the replacement of utility theory by the model we outlined would cause them no end of problems" Amos Tversky letter to Paul Slovic*[23]"

---

23   Michael Lewis, *The Undoing Project*, 2017, W. W. Norton Company, page 378

Conclusion

There is ample evidence that the Law of Demand and the associated curve fails to provide scientific proof of any economic theory and has no application in real life. However, the theories have a stubborn persistence that is not easy to explain:

> "Why has economics persisted with a theory which has been comprehensively shown to be unsound? Why, despite the destructive impact of economic policies, does economics continue to be the toolkit which politicians and bureaucrats apply to almost all social and economic issues?"[24]

One possible reason is the theories are related to social engineering goals that have nothing to do with science or truth, but instead are related to goals of politicians and bureaucrats. More on that thought later.

---

24 Steven Keen, *Debunking Economics*, Zed Books, 2011, page xv

CHAPTER 4
Market Pricing

The First Law of Economists: For every economist, there exists an equal and opposite economist.

The Second Law of Economists: They're both wrong.

—David Wildasin, Professor Economics

THIS CHAPTER INTRODUCES a more realistic view of one of the most important questions for economists; how is a price determined? The view offered is very dynamic, and most importantly, based upon observations.

Market Pricing

Any consumer can review prices they have paid over the last few months, identifying various situations where the price seemed great or not so great. This simple observation clearly shows that prices can operate over a wide range. Three rules seem appropriate for describing the experience.

1. The price for a product can cover a range of values from below cost to as high as anyone will pay. Even though a price below cost is possible, it is not sustainable, and will only last for brief periods. (i.e.

post-Christmas sales, going out of business sales, etc.)

2. The more market influence a supplier has, the higher the price they will obtain.

3. The more market influence a buyer has, the lower the price they will pay.

There can be several factors that affect market influence. Generally, the same factor either leans towards the supplier or the buyer. Consider the following the six market factors affecting relative influence and price. (See figure 1)

Parent's Wisdom

These six items are well known to parents who have shopped for all types of items, such as cars, houses, groceries, and various

Factors Determining Market Influence/Pricing	Favors Consumer	Favors Seller
Choice: Number of Competitors Similar Competing Products	More Choices Easy for firms to Enter Market	Fewer Choices: Patent Protection, Constrained Markets, New Products
Perceived Need: Maslow's Hierarchy Emotional Leverage	Want vs Need Lack of Emotional Appeal	Must Have (for any reason)
Knowledge: Simplicity or Complexity Frequent or Infrequent Use	Simple, familiar, frequent use Ability to learn traits	Complex, infrequent use
Time Factors	Spoilage motivates seller	Sense of Urgency for buyer
Personal Power	Assertive Personality	Skilled Salesmanship
Variations in Flow	Surplus	Scarcity

Ch 4 Figure 1 – Six Factors Affecting Market Price

services. Students who have not gained experience acquiring goods and services will be unaware of these subtleties. A student is easily swayed when told that price is driven by supply and demand.

What is supply and demand? Economists will tell you it is quantity supplied at a price and quantity demanded at a price. Focusing on quantity and price completely misses the depth of human behavior. The first market factor is choice, which is similar to supply for an economist. Examining only quantity leaves out color, style, design etc. The economist view of a market is sterile, leaving nothing behind but products one might find in a communist market place, all shoes are the same style and color.

The second market factor is perceived need, which is similar to demand for an economist. By examining only quantity, the economist once again bleaches out the vigor of what actually occurs in the market. Due to this sterile view, marketing is hardly addressed in an economics class. In reality, marketing efforts are ingrained in day to day life activity. Hardly a moment goes by without a commercial or ad.

Parents need to coach their students on how to read a market. Just like teaching your child how to fish for trout involves reading the ripples on the surface, learning how to shop involves reading the market for conditions that benefit the buyer.

As an example, parents know that shopping for a car at the end of a season may present opportunities to save, due to variations in flow, i.e., surplus of last year's inventory. There may also be time pressures to complete sales before the end of the year for a firm to achieve a sales quota.

On a broader scale, consider the health care market, which scores high on several factors that favor the seller.

1. Perceived Need—Healthcare is high on perceived need.

2. Knowledge—Healthcare is a complex product.

3. Choice—Few patients consider they have a choice. Patents restrict choice on critical life-saving drugs. Healthcare is a very constrained market, with pricing set by insurance companies and providers. It is nearly impossible to call a hospital for a quote on a procedure. *Time Magazine*'s article, *Bitter Pill,* clearly paints a picture of a tiered pricing that actually puts the poorest people at the greatest disadvantage.

4. Time—Time for treating an illness can be critical for health or even survival.

These four factors, along with market imperfections, have led to a steady increase in healthcare costs over the last twenty years in the USA. The percent GDP for healthcare has risen from 8% to 16%, while the rest of the western world has risen from about 8% to 11% of GDP. The rest of the western world has identified healthcare as a product that is subject to factors that produce excessive prices, and have taken steps to constrain the markets.

Dynamic Market Pricing

These observations lead to a model that has a range of available prices. Prices are not quantity dependent. They are not driven by supply and demand curves, but are influenced by the six factors introduced earlier. The old terms supply and demand are contained in the model as captured by the concept of choices and needs. Stable markets operate over a period of time without experiencing a surplus or shortage. During these times, the amount of product produced and purchased stays fairly constant, avoiding surplus or scarcity.

Consider a slowdown in the real estate market, where the

number of buyers drops considerably. The market is now viewed as a buyer's market as buyers have more choices than usual. A surplus is created as sellers are taking longer to find buyers. In the end, the price agreed to by the parties will be affected by the factors shown. For example, if the buying party develops an emotional attachment to a particular house, they will pay a higher price than someone that would be indifferent towards that one house.

The idea that price is determined in a mechanical process that relies solely on quantity is far too simple to describe what actually occurs.

Price Distribution

A good way to view pricing for different market conditions is to consider a distribution function that varies in shape, based upon the type of market and how the six factors favor either buyers or sellers. Consider the figure 2:

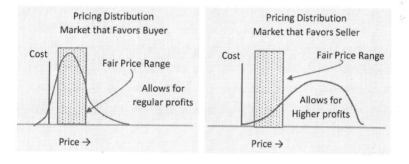

Ch 4 Figure 2 – Price Distribution – Fair Pricing vs High Profit Pricing

The first chart shows a distribution that is closer to cost than the second chart. A fair pricing range is a price that provides adequate, but not excessive, profits. The more influence a firm has in the market, the higher the profits will be. Firms like Mylan Pharmacuetical have obscene profits, with products that are priced excessivley high, due to excess influence in the market. Much of this excess influence has been purchased from Congress, which then provides favorable legislation or lax regulation that promotes the firm's influence. With the increased influence, the firm becomes the architect for their own markets, removiang any semblence of compettion.

Pricing is an extremely dynamic process, dependent upon market factors that either favor the consumer or the supplier. There is no one measure of price in a market. Even an average price can be misleading if the data is skewed or the products vary considerably. An economics class today avoids teaching the reality of the markets and hides the price gouging that Americans experience every day.

Historic Perspectives

Prior to the days of Adam Smith, a fair price or natural price was referred to as a just price, as taught by Scholasticism. Scholasticism was a method of critical thought promoted by academics from various universities across Europe from the 1100s to the 1700s. Thomas Aquinas was perhaps the most widely known Scholastic. In his most famous work, *Summa Theologica*, he attempted to address the definition of a just price, with two steps:

1. Common Advantage:

    Whether it was lawful to sell a thing for more than its worth? Buying and selling seem to be established for the common advantage of both parties, one of whom requires that which belongs to the other, and vice versa ... Now, whatever is established for the common advantage should not be more of a burden to one party than to another . . .

2.   Adequate Living

The Scholastics conclude that a merchant is entitled to sell at a profit, assuming the profits are adequate to provide the merchant's necessities for living. The price that provides the merchant with the necessities of life is a just price. Anything over a just price would provide excess wealth over and above one's normal needs and would be considered avarice. (Profiting at extreme levels was once a sin against Christianity and one's fellow man.)

Notice the Scholastics left out the factor of quantity. Without knowing quantity sold, total profits cannot be determined. The idea that the percent mark-up on a product sold could be the judge of a fair price, does not properly capture the idea of adequate profits. The idea is more complex than the Scholastics thought.

During the Middle Ages and the Renaissance, the Catholic Church, with scholastic teachings on price, could have a significant impact on society. The Christian courts could punish merchants for greedy behavior. The punishment could be fines or even excommunication, which in the 12th century would be tantamount to expulsion from society. Here is an example from the year 1635, in Boston.[25]

---

25   Robert L. Heilbroner, "The Worldly Philosophers—The Lives, Times and Ideas of the Great Economic Thinkers" 7th edition, Simon and Schuster 1995, pg 15

"A trial is in progress; one Robert Keayne, "an ancient professor of the gospel, a man of eminent parts, wealthy and having but one child, and having come over for conscience' sake and for the advancement of the gospel," is charged with a heinous crime: he has made over sixpence profit on the shilling, an outrageous gain. *(A shilling was equal to 12 pence—thus a 50% mark-up.) Author's clarification.* The court is debating whether to excommunicate him for his sin; but, in view of his spotless past, it finally relents and dismisses him with a fine of two hundred pounds. But poor Mr. Keayne is so upset that, before the elders of the Church, he does "with tears acknowledge his covetous and corrupt heart." The minister of Boston cannot resist this golden opportunity to profit from the living example of a wayward sinner, and he uses the example of Keayne's avarice to thunder forth in his Sunday sermon on some false principles of trade. Among them are these:

1. That a man might sell as dear as he can, and buy as cheap as he can.

2. If a man lose by casualty of sea, etc., in some of his commodities, he may raise the price of the rest.

3. That he may sell as he bought, though he paid too dear . . .

All false, false, false, cries the minister; to seek riches for riches' sake is to fall into the sin of avarice."

This type of intervention had a chilling effect on commerce. It took several hundred years for the church to relax their views on profits (and usury) and allow free commerce to achieve great gains for society.

Adam Smith was keenly aware of the influence of the church

and the scholastics that operated from the universities that were founded by the church.

> "The present universities of Europe were originally, the greater part of them, ecclesiastical corporations, instituted for the education of churchmen. They were founded by the authority of the Pope, and were so entirely under his protection . . . . What was taught in the greater part of these universities was suitable to the ends of their institution." [26]

Wealth of Nations was a book that assisted in moving western culture away from the ideas of the Scholastics and towards the ideas of free commerce, without the stringent restraints of the past.

The most liberating aspect of Adam Smith's classical economics was removing the idea of judgement or ethics from the process of commerce. Markets became regulators of price, not the local church. The invisible hand supposedly assured that self-interest would be turned to the good of all society:

> "He intends only his own gain, and he is in this, as in many other cases, led by an invisible hand to promote an end which no part of intention. . . . By pursuing his own interest, he frequently promotes that of society more effectually than when he really intends to promote it." [27]

Adam Smith lived in the day of shopkeepers, farmers and merchants. The industrial revolution was in its infancy and

---

26 Adam Smith, Wealth of Nations, Metilibri, digital edition, 2007 page 592

27 Ibid page 349

markets were predominantly served by small individual businesses that were suppliers and participants on the local community. Monopolies were considered anomalies to the market and existed usually at the will of the king or national government. The East India Company was one of the first corporations, and was born when chartered by Queen Elizabeth in the early 1600s as a monopoly.

Consider the excerpt from "The Worldy Philosophers" by *Robert L. Heilbroner*

"The world of Adam Smith has been called a world of atomistic competition, a world in which no agent of the productive mechanism, on the side of labor or capital, was powerful enough to interfere with or to resist the pressures of competition."[28]

Heilbroner then questions the assumption of atomistic competition.

"And today? Does the competitive market mechanism still operate? This is not a question to which it is possible to give a simple answer. The nature of the market has changed vastly since the eighteenth century. We no longer live in a world of atomistic competition in which no man can afford to swim against the current. Today's market mechanism is characterized by the huge size of its participants: giant corporations and strong labor unions obviously do not behave as if they were individual proprietors and workers. Their very bulk enables them to stand out against the pressures of competition, to disregard

---

28   Robert L Heilbroner, Ibid page 36

price signals, and to consider what their self-interest shall be in the long run rather than in the immediate press of each day's buying and selling."[29]

The individual entrepreneurs of the past have been replaced by corporations that do not have the same sense of brotherhood and community that existed in Adam Smith's time. Corporations do not experience the social pressures of a Christian community that tend to curb avarice. In fact, economists have claimed that a corporation's sole social responsibility is to promote profits:

"The social responsibility of business is to increase its profits"[30]

The easiest way for an American Corporation to increase profits today is to cut salary expenses by moving production out of the country. The idea of global competition through a mechanism other than trade was beyond Adam Smith's ability to predict.

Adam Smith was unable to see how corporations would be exempt from social pressures.

"The corn merchant himself is likely to suffer the most by his excess of avarice, not only from the indignation which it generally excites against him."[31]

Indignation from the community will have absolutely no

---

29   ibid

30   Milton Friedman, The Social Responsibility of Business is to Increase its Profits, *New York Times Magazine*, September 13, 1970

31   "Wealth of Nations" page 550

effect on corporations or the executives that run them. Without social pressure, there is no compelling reason for a corporation to price a product fairly, once it has a strong market position. Corporations are following Milton Friedman's prescription of increasing profits at all costs.

Corporations will constantly look for ways to move the market factors to a position that favors the seller. Extending the life of a patent is a prime example. Paying study groups to support the corporate view, followed by lobbying Congress, is a common tactic. A classic example is an article published in *Journal of Health Economics,* which was developed by Tufts Center for the study of drug development. The study concluded the cost of developing a single drug in 2003 was $800 million. They have updated the study several times, and now claim the cost is $2.5 billion to develop a new drug. This single report shows up as a reference many times in different publications, including *Scientific American.* Considering that the Tufts Center is a think tank that receives most of its grant money from biomedical firms is enough to question the results of the study. Here are a few quotes from *The Washington Post,* which ran a story on these estimates . . . (By Jason Millman November 18, 2014)

> "James Love, director of the non-profit Knowledge Ecology International, said critical information is missing from the analysis, like how many patients were in the drug trials, or how much money was claimed to have been spent on each patient. "First impression: the study, which is part of a public relations campaign by the drug companies to justify high prices, is long on propaganda, and short of details,"

. . . .

Doctors Without Borders was harsher in its assessment. "[If] you believe [the Tufts analysis], you probably also believe the earth is flat," said policy director Rohit Malpani.

. . . .

Merrill Goozner, in his book "The $800 Million Pill: The Truth Behind the Cost of New Drugs," writes that the actual development cost was about one-fifth of the last Tufts estimate, contending that most of the drug development relies on taxpayer-funded research.

For more information on how corporations purchase lobbying material from major universities, read "Leasing the Ivory Tower, the corporate takeover of academia" by Lawrence C. Soley.

Let there be no doubt, prices are not determined by supply and demand curves. They are determined by the factors identified above. Every supplier will use these factors to command the highest price possible.

Conclusion:

Economics taught today is a foil to obscure the true factors that determine pricing in markets. The theories serve the benefit of owners and profiteers by hiding profits and unjust pricing. A true free market would not be dominated by firms created through mergers and acquisitions that reduce choice and concentrate power in fewer hands. If Teddy Roosevelt were to walk the halls of Congress today, he would be stunned to find the return of "Trusts", in the form of mega-corporations, aided by lobbyists stomping triumphantly through the halls of Congress, ruling America as if democracy did not exist.

Supply and Demand curves fail to explain price increases for Mylan Pharmaceuticals. Yet, Mylan's CEO, Heather Bresch, uses supply and demand to cloud the issue and avoid any repercussions. From an interview on CNBC: (8/15/2016)

CNBC: "Are the price hikes done?"

Heather Bresch: "We are going to continue to run a business. And we are going to continue to meet the supply and demand that is out there."

Heather never mentions the following;

1. The lobbying effort that resulted in laws that encourage and require schools to maintain a stock of auto injectors.

2. The near monopoly the firm holds by virtue of a patent they purchased from Merck in 2007.

3. The amount of debt the firm has taken on to support several leveraged buy outs and the added interest expense the firm must now pay.

The price has nothing to do with supply and demand. The price for an epipen has increased dramatically from $120 in 2009 to $609 in 2016 in order to help Mylan pay for acquisitions. Mylan borrowed approximately $14 billion from 2007 through 2016 to acquire various firms. The interest rate on the debt ranges from 3-7% creating an annual expense of $455 million. In addition to the interest expense, somehow the $14 billion in debt will need to be paid off. Through this time, the CEO pay for Heather Bresch grew from $2.4 million to $18.9 million.

CHAPTER 5

Economic Card Tricks

Framing theory suggests that how something is presented to the audience (called "the frame") influences the choices people make about how to process that information. [32]

THIS CHAPTER REVEALS the mathematical errors and sleight of hand used by economists when discussing a sub-field of economics referred to as Marginalism. Three different card tricks will be exposed:

1. Marginal Cost—The mathematical foundation for the supply curve

2. Marginal Product of Labor—The mathematical foundation for the labor-demand curve, and the theory that minimum wage causes unemployment.

3. Marginal Revenue—The mathematical foundation for two key economic models, monopoly and monopolistic competition.

---

32 Erving Goffman, Fame Analysis, Northeastern University Press, 1986. While Goffman initiated the ideas around framing theory, the quote above came from https://masscommtheory.com/theory-overviews/framing-theory/

Economists claim their mathematics justify their theories. Unfortunately, once the card tricks are revealed, all a reader sees is a weak attempt to fool the unsuspecting.

To receive the full benefit of this chapter, a reader should have a good grasp of high school mathematics. If math is not a strong suit, partnering with someone will help and likely provide an entertaining discussion as to why someone would go to such extremes.

Marginal Cost

In Chapter 2 of this book, the topic of fabricated data for variable cost was introduced. Variable cost, as taught in Mankiw's *Economics*, follows a quadratic relationship.

$$variable \frac{cost}{cup} = 0.1(\# \ of \ cups)^2 + 0.2(\# \ of \ cups)$$

Mankiw uses this relationship to promote the misconception of rising marginal costs, and proposes that all typical firms must address this issue.[33] (See figure 1)

"Many firms experience increasing marginal product before diminishing marginal product. As a result, they have cost curves shaped like those in the figure."

In reality, a rising marginal cost curve has never been seen in any business. It is not typical. In-fact, this curve is mathematically inconsistent with normal business practices.

---

33 Gregory Mankiw, *Principles of Economics* 6th edition published 2012 by South-Western, Cengage Learning page 271

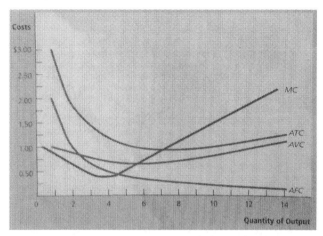

Ch 5 Figure 1 – Mankiw Cost Curves

Framing Theory

The first part of a card trick is the observer's preconceived notion of a deck of cards. Observers expect a deck of cards to have 52 cards, four suits, and 13 cards in each suit. In economic modeling, the framing for the card trick is a set of accounting data and the associated break-even graph. (See figure 2)

The table of data contains six typical accounting measures for running a business.

1. Quantity—the number of items manufactured during an accounting period. (A typical accounting period is one month.)

2. Fixed Costs—such as rent, which are fixed for the accounting period.

3. Variable Costs—the costs for labor and materials consumed in the manufacture of one item.

4. Total Variable Costs—As more items are produced, this is the sum of all variable costs for those items during the accounting period.

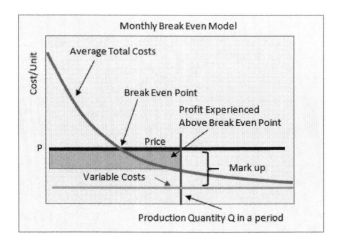

Quantity	Fixed Costs	Variable Costs	Total Variable Costs	Total costs	Average Total Costs
1	$ 100	$ 13	$ 13	$ 113	$ 113
2	$ 100	$ 13	$ 26	$ 126	$ 63
3	$ 100	$ 13	$ 39	$ 139	$ 46
4	$ 100	$ 13	$ 52	$ 152	$ 38
5	$ 100	$ 13	$ 65	$ 165	$ 33
6	$ 100	$ 13	$ 78	$ 178	$ 30
7	$ 100	$ 13	$ 91	$ 191	$ 27
8	$ 100	$ 13	$ 104	$ 204	$ 26
9	$ 100	$ 13	$ 117	$ 217	$ 24
10	$ 100	$ 13	$ 130	$ 230	$ 23

Ch 5 Figure 2 – Accounting Break Even Model

5. Total Costs—the sum of fixed costs and total variable costs.

6. Average Total Costs—Total costs divided by number of units manufactured

Three of these items, variable costs, average total costs, and price, are combined to make the break-even chart. The concept of a breakeven chart is a common topic for an introductory business class. A student learns how increasing the quantity sold in a month helps to increase profits by lowering average costs and garnering more revenue. The area in the shaded rectangle represents profits for a given quantity of items sold.

Frame Distortion

The economist takes the familiar framework and distorts the foundation. A comparison of the six items in the accountant's model and the six items in an economist's model reveals the first keys to the card trick. The items with a solid arrows have not changed, while items with a dashed arrow have been renamed. (See figure 3)

1. "Variable Costs" are now called "Marginal Costs per Unit" or marginal costs.

2. Total variable costs are now labeled as variable costs.

The purpose of the renaming is to confuse people. The primary goal is to make a person think there is a new measure called "marginal cost." With the new name, marginal cost can easily be given new properties that have never before been associated with variable costs. When "Total" is removed from the column for total variable costs, a student will have a difficult time recognizing that Variable Costs are actually the total of the marginal costs values in column five. The level of confusion

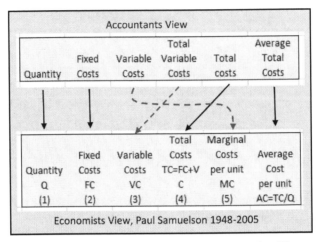

Ch 5 Figure 3 – Accountants View vs Economists View

caused by the new names is extremely high. Even accountants are unaware that the cards of the deck have been manipulated.

The economist goes to great lengths to legitimize marginal cost as something new, by creating an elaborate description of how marginal cost is calculated. The table of data has extra rows provided to support calculating the new value, marginal cost. (See figure 4) From Mankiw's textbook:

"Marginal cost per unit is very important. MC is the "extra cost" that comes from producing an "extra unit of Q." You get it by subtracting from new larger TC the previous TC you had when you were producing one less unit (Important: check column (5) to verify your understanding of this)." [34]

---

34 Paul Samuelson, *Economics: An Introductory Analysis* (New York, McGraw-Hill Book Company, 1958) page 461

Quantity Q (1)	Fixed Costs FC (2)	Variable Costs VC (3)	Total Cost TC = FC + VC (4)	Marginal Cost per unit MC (5)	Average cost per unit AC=TC/Q
0	256	0	256		***
				64	
1	256	64	320		320
				20	
2	256	84	340		170
				15	
3	256	99	355		118
				13	
4	256	112	368		92
				13	
5	256	125	381		76
				19	
6	256	144	400		67
				31	
7	256	175	431		62
				49	
8	256	224	480		60
				73	
9	256	297	553		61
				103	
10	256	400	656		66

Ch 5 Figure 4 – Misdirection

A magician refers to this technique as misdirection. By driving the participant's attention at a specific item, they fail to see other items that would be suspect and reveal the trick. This technique has been used in textbooks for over sixty years, and no one has ever asked why the variable cost column is now the total of marginal costs or what is the difference between marginal cost and variable cost?

The economist's descriptions compound the confusion by using further tactics:

1. Use long, complicated descriptions, with new and unfamiliar vocabulary.

   a. *"Column one indicates the different levels of production per unit time, going from 0 up to 10 units."* What is meant by levels of production? The column is labeled quantity. Isn't quantity just the number of units produced?

2. Leave out clarifying information.

   a. The variable costs column is actually total variable costs or in this distorted frame total marginal cost.

3. Add information that isn't necessary.

   a. The description "Average Total Cost per unit" is redundant. Average already implies a cost per unit.

4. Misuse of terms.

   a. Marginal Costs "per unit" implies an average of some sort; but, this number is not an average value. Marginal cost is defined as the cost to produce the next unit, or the nth unit.

Once a student has been thoroughly confused by the introduction, the textbook continues to describe the shape of curves that are typically portrayed in an economic model.[35]

---

35 On Line Course Material University of Idaho, Econ272 *Foundations of Economic Analysis* Text:—Jon R. Miller—http://www.webpages. uidaho.edu/econ272/online_text/master_all_4th_ed.pdf

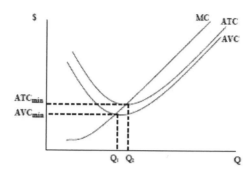

Ch 5 Figure 5 – Elegant Curves

(See figure 5) However, the economist has stacked the deck by fabricating the data for marginal cost. Since the student is not familiar with the term marginal cost, he trusts the teacher's authority and accepts the description of constantly increasing marginal cost as a proven observation by economic scientists. In reality, no one has ever seen a cost that behaves in this manner.

This use of fabricated data is made possible by renaming variable costs as marginal cost. Variable costs are a familiar quantity for business owners and accountants. Variable costs are known to stay fairly constant. The reason variable costs are fairly constant is related to the acquisition method for materials for production. When a manufacturer makes hundreds of items, the inputs are purchased in bulk. The bulk purchase sets a fixed variable cost for that factor of production for hundreds of units. Variable costs do not change from the 20th item to the 21st, and Marginal Costs do not change from the 20th item to the 21st.

The card trick works every time. Students will believe there is a concept called marginal cost that is different from variable costs, when, in fact, these concepts are identical.

Challenging the economists

One simple challenge to the economist is a question about production costs for the 10th item. According to the table, the 10th item will have a variable cost of $103. (See figure 6) However, instead of producing the 10th item at the end of the month, if production of the 10th item is delayed to the next accounting period, the firm is producing the 1st item of the next month, and the variable cost drops to $64. Why would production costs drop by delaying production?

There is no explanation for this odd behavior for costs. Economists duck this question by referring back to the vague description of column one;

Quantity Q (1)	Variable Costs for nth unit (5)
1	$ 64
2	$ 20
3	$ 15
4	$ 13
5	$ 13
6	$ 19
7	$ 31
8	$ 49
9	$ 73
10	$ 103

Ch 5 Figure 6

> . . . indicates the different levels of production per unit time . . .

However, column one is titled quantity, nothing to do with per unit time.

This simple question exposed the trick that Paul Samuelson had developed for his textbooks. Given the concern that the card trick would no longer work as math skills improved at the high school level, economists had to modify the card trick.

Their fix can be called rate switching.

Gregory Mankiw's Rate Switch

In 2005, Gregory Mankiw replaced Paul Samuelson as the primary author for introductory economic books. Mr. Mankiw

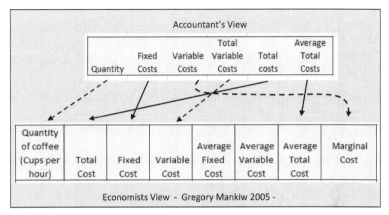

Ch 5 Figure 7 – Rates of Production

responded to the previous challenge by slightly changing his data. (See figure 7)

Mankiw kept the first two changes related to marginal cost and variable cost, but modified his quantity to be a rate or quantity per hour.

With this change, Mankiw prevents skeptical questions about deferring production to the next accounting period.

For most people, it is difficult to tell the difference between a quantity and a rate. After the time period has passed, wouldn't quantity and rate be the same? Mankiw's disguise is clever, but not clever enough. There are two avenues of thought that reveal the flaw of using a rate instead of a quantity. (See figure 8)

1. Fixed cost is related to an accounting time period. Typically, the accounting period is a month. By specifying a rate per hour, the time period is now an hour, and any fixed costs would be for an hour. Mankiw never explains the $3.00 per hour fixed costs. Failing to clarify is a strategy for creating

Quantity of coffee (Cups per hour)	Total Cost	Fixed Cost	Variable Cost	Average Fixed Cost	Average Variable Cost	Average Total Cost	Marginal Cost
0	$ 3.00	$ 3.00	$ -				
							$ 0.30
1	$ 3.30	$ 3.00	$ 0.30	$ 3.00	$ 0.30	$ 3.30	
							$ 0.50
2	$ 3.80	$ 3.00	$ 0.80	$ 1.50	$ 0.40	$ 1.90	
							$ 0.70
3	$ 4.50	$ 3.00	$ 1.50	$ 1.00	$ 0.50	$ 1.50	
							$ 0.90
4	$ 5.40	$ 3.00	$ 2.40	$ 0.75	$ 0.60	$ 1.35	
							$ 1.10
5	$ 6.50	$ 3.00	$ 3.50	$ 0.60	$ 0.70	$ 1.30	
							$ 1.30
6	$ 7.80	$ 3.00	$ 4.80	$ 0.50	$ 0.80	$ 1.30	
							$ 1.50
7	$ 9.30	$ 3.00	$ 6.30	$ 0.43	$ 0.90	$ 1.33	
							$ 1.70
8	$ 11.00	$ 3.00	$ 8.00	$ 0.38	$ 1.00	$ 1.38	
							$ 1.90
9	$ 12.90	$ 3.00	$ 9.90	$ 0.33	$ 1.10	$ 1.43	
							$ 2.10
10	$ 15.00	$ 3.00	$ 12.00	$ 0.30	$ 1.20	$ 1.50	

Ch5 Figure 8 – Mankiw Data for Rates of Production

confusion. If the accounting period is an hour, would labor costs now be considered fixed, since staff is paid by the hour? Given that rent is a monthly expense, the rental fixed costs would depend upon how many hours the store operates in a month. This is a significant distortion from the framework of a break-even model.

2. Rates are not the same as amounts. Without time, there is no quantity. Mankiw never specifies the number of hours of production. The result is mathematical gibberish.

The mathematical difference between rates and amounts.

At this point, a student of pre-cal or physics could be your best partner. They will have already learned how to graph functions of time where rate is the slope of a line.

The easiest way to clarify the difference between a rate and amount is to consider speed and distance. If someone is told to drive at 30 mile per hour, there is no way to know how far the person has driven unless the duration of the trip is also known. With a rate of quantity per hour, you must also know time to know quantity produced. If the amount of time is not specified, there is no way to understand costs or other business measures. Given that Mankiw's coffee shop can run at different rates through the day, it is impossible to show what happens for an entire day.

Consider the story of the race between the tortoise and the hare. The tortoise travelled at a steady pace. The hare ran fast, goofed off, and ran fast again, but was beaten by the tortoise. The race can be modeled with a graph of distance and time. (See figure 9)

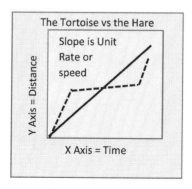

Ch 5 Figure 9 – Tortoise Vs: Hare

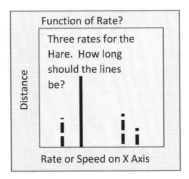

Ch 5 Figure 10 – Can't Use Rate

The single straight line represents the tortoise travelling at a constant rate. The dashed lines represent the hare running at three different rates.

Ask your student to change the x axis to rate and attempt to represent distance traveled on the y axis. They will tell you it is impossible to draw a line to represent the distance travelled as a function of speed for either the rabbit or the hare. (See figure 10) In this graph, the solid line represents the tortoise traveling at a constant rate. The line simply points straight up as the speed is constant. The other dashed lines represent the different speeds at which the Hare was running; but without the time for each rate, it is not clear how far the Hare travelled.

It is impossible to graph a function with a rate on the x axis and distance on the Y axis. However, the economist uses this framework to complete the card trick with three quick steps.

Step 1: Assume the coffee shop operates at one hour for each of the possible rates. This creates a family of 10 vertical lines showing how costs grow as the hour progresses for each of the ten different rates. (See figure 11)

Step 2: Draw a line through the dots and erase the family of vertical lines. (See figure 12)

Quantity of coffee (Cups per hour)	Total Cost
0	$ 3.00
1	$ 3.30
2	$ 3.80
3	$ 4.50
4	$ 5.40
5	$ 6.50
6	$ 7.80
7	$ 9.30
8	$ 11.00
9	$ 12.90
10	$ 15.00

Creating a function of a Rate

Total Cost for One Hour

Ch 5 Figure 11 – Mankiw's How to fabricate a function

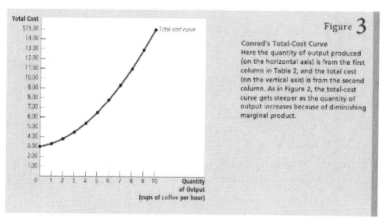

Total Cost

Figure **3**

Conrad's Total-Cost Curve
Here the quantity of output produced (on the horizontal axis) is from the first column in Table 2, and the total cost (on the vertical axis) is from the second column. As in Figure 2, the total-cost curve gets steeper as the quantity of output increases because of diminishing marginal product.

Quantity of Output (cups of coffee per hour)

Ch 5 Figure 12 – Mankiw's Fabricated Cost for cups and cups per hour

Step 3: Sew more confusion by referring to the X-Axis as quantity of output and rates of output at the same time.[36]

The economist has transformed a family of dots relating rates and costs into a graph of cost as a function of quantity. Or is it a function of quantity per hour?

Your high school students should be vigorously shaking their heads and saying, "no way".

Challenging the Economist

Earlier in this chapter, the logical challenge involved asking why the 10th item of production would cost less if the item was delayed to the next accounting period and became the first item of production. In a similar fashion, why would the 10th item in an hour cost $2.10, while delaying production to the next hour would drop its cost to $0.30? (See figure 13)

What is the meaning of marginal cost when discussing rates? According to Mankiw's glossary:

"Marginal cost is the increase in total cost that arises from an extra unit of production."

If someone is making eight cups per hour, does that mean that each cup costs an extra $1.70? If so, total costs would be (8 x $1.70 + $3.00 = $16.60) for the hour not $11.00 as shown in the table. The only explanation that makes sense is that marginal cost in this table is the difference between making different batches of coffee at different rates. In effect, four cups in an hour cost $5.40, and five cups in an hour cost $6.50, the difference

---

36   Gregory Mankiw, *Economics* 6th Edition, Southwestern-Cengage, Pg 267 Figure 3

Quantity of coffee (Cups per hour)	Total Cost	Marginal Cost
0	$ 3.00	
1	$ 3.30	$ 0.30
2	$ 3.80	$ 0.50
3	$ 4.50	$ 0.70
4	$ 5.40	$ 0.90
5	$ 6.50	$ 1.10
6	$ 7.80	$ 1.30
7	$ 9.30	$ 1.50
8	$ 11.00	$ 1.70
9	$ 12.90	$ 1.90
10	$ 15.00	$ 2.10

Ch 5 Figure 13 – Marginal Cost

would be $1.10. This is not consistent with the definition of marginal cost from Mankiw's glossary.

The truth is the concept of marginal cost for the next cup of coffee cannot be represented using a table of data based upon rates of production.

It is safe to say that most high school students who are college bound can follow this explanation. Just as assuredly, Paul Samuelson who graduated from Harvard with a David Wells award, should be aware of this mathematical error as well. Later, in Chapter 8, it will become evident how economic experts are trapped and blinded by their ideology and are unable to find true knowledge behind their curves.

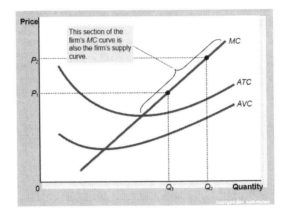

Ch 5 Figure 14 – Marginal Cost

Purpose of Card Trick

The reason this card trick is so important is that economic theory proposes the marginal cost curve is the mathematical justification for the upward-sloping supply curve. (See figure 14) Once the card trick is rejected, the student refers back to the accountant's break-even model and concludes that variable costs are flat and supply curves must be flat.

In mathematics, a flat curve means that one variable does not affect the other. Since factors of production are bought in bulk, it has to be true that variable costs do not change as quantity produced increases from one unit to the next. It could be true that the next batch is more expensive, but it would not be represented in this fashion.

Elements of the Card Trick

1. Renaming variable costs to marginal costs. They are in fact the same thing.

2. Fabricating data to make it appear marginal costs increase with increases in production quantity. This type of cost behavior has never been seen in a true production environment.

3. Misuse of mathematical graphs by using rates as the x-axis.

4. Moving back and forth between rates and quantities as values on the x-axis.

Most people who have not been trained in mathematics would never catch these tricks. That is the beauty of the deception. Predominantly, the only people capable of catching the deception are those who work in academia.

Marginal Product of Labor—Card Trick #2

"The genius of a great magician is as impressive as the genius of a great scientist."

—Amit Kalantri

This chapter explores the economic concept of marginal product of labor, and once again shows how economists are either confused about basic math or they are performing a card trick to confuse their students.

Framing

The frame for this trick is once again the typical mathematical function. Consider the functional relationship between miles driven and gas consumed. The value of miles driven increases from left to right and the value of gas increases from bottom to top. The property of <u>sequential dependence</u> requires that, in

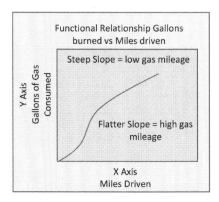

Ch 5 Figure 15 – Functional Graph

order to drive three miles, one must have already driven two miles. The input is the x-axis variable, and the output is the y-axis variable. When students see a graph, they assume it has these same properties. (See figure 15)

Production Function

Gregory Mankiw introduces the "Production Function"[37] with a table of data. (See figure 16) He describes the first two columns as follows:

> "When there is 1 worker, she produces 50 cookies. When there are 2 workers, she produces 90 cookies. . . . the marginal product is shown halfway between two rows because it represents the change in output as the number of workers increases from one level to another."

---

37   Gregory Mankiw, *Economics*, Sixth Edition, South-Western Cengage Learning,20123 page 263

(1)	(2)	(3)	(4)	(5)	(6)
Number Of Worlers	Output (Quantity of cookies prodiced per hour)	Marginal Product of Labor	Cost of Factory	Cost of Workers	Total Cost of Inputs (Cost of factory + cost of workers)
0	0		30	0	30
		50			
1	50		30	10	40
		40			
2	90		30	20	50
		30			
3	120		30	30	60
		20			
4	140		30	40	70
		10			
5	150		30	50	80
		5			
6	155		30	60	90

Ch 5 Figure 16 – Data for Mankiw's Production Function

Mankiw then uses the data from columns one, two, and six to create the following two graphs. (See figure 17) The economist presents the data as if it were a normal function. The number of workers hired determines the quantity of output. This sounds like the logical framing of a function.

However, this is not the deck of cards it appears to be. Taking a closer look reveals:

1. The output is not a quantity; it is a rate. (Cookies per hour)

2. The input is not person hours, but size of team. The number of workers hired is a choice of the hiring manager, who can select any of six different team sizes at the start of production. A labor input must be person hours.

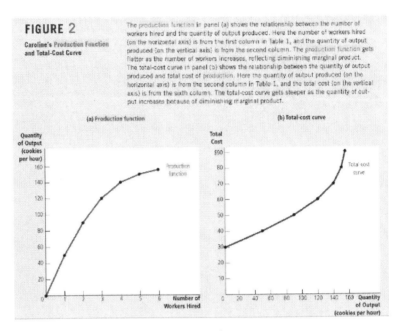

Ch 5 Figure 17 – Fake Functions

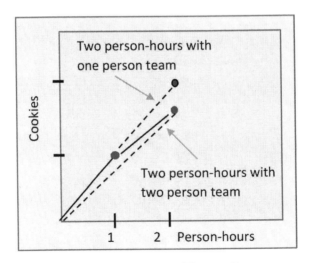

Ch 5 Figure 18 – Person Hours as Input

Without a specified time, there are no person hours and there is no production.

One critical question reveals the card trick. What would happen if the one-person team worked two hours? The answer is the extended dashed line showing one worker producing 100 cookies. This also reveals the second dashed line reflecting the reduced productivity of the two-person team producing only 90 cookies. The one person team is more productive! (See figure 18)

Proper View of Labor and Rates of Production

To completely unravel the card trick, a mathematician's or engineer's view of the data is required. (See figure 19)

1. Column 1—Number of Workers on a team. Economic production is not dependent upon the number of workers, but instead dependent upon the

(1)	(2)	(3)	(4)
Number Of Worlers	Productivity Cookies per Hour	Productivity Cookies per Man Hour	Cookies Produced with Six Man Hours of Production
1	50	50	300
2	90	45	270
3	120	40	240
4	140	35	210
5	150	30	180
6	155	25.8	155

Ch 5 Figure 19 – Corrected Data for Production Function

product of workers and time, commonly referred to as person-hours.

2. Column 2 is the same data from Mankiw, but instead of an amount of cookies, it is properly viewed as a rate of output for various-sized work teams. This is best described as a productivity measure, measured in cookies per hour.

3. A new column 3 shows the productivity per person for each different team size. This is found by dividing rate of cookies for the team by the number of team members. (Value = Col 2 / Col 1)

4. The last column is a measure of production for each team, assuming each team consumed six man-hours of labor. (Value = Col 3 x 6 hours)

Correcting for the deceptions leads to the following interpretation of quantity produced as a function of person-hours. (See figure 20)

1. The straight lines represent the production possibilities, based upon team size and person hours consumed. The slope of the line is a measure of productivity. The steeper the slope, the higher the productivity.

2. The hiring manager can either have production teams of 1, 2, 3, 4, 5 or 6 people working. If the production manager is not time constrained, he hires one worker as a one person team has the highest productivity. If he needs to produce a certain number of cookies in an hour, he may hire more workers.

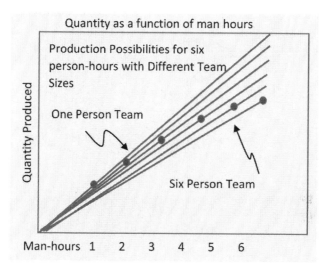

Ch 5 Figure 20 – Production Possibilities based on team size

Comparing the original table of data to the data in the new graph, we see that the original quantity produced was for one hour for each team. The dots show the quantity produced for each team, assuming one hour has gone by. The correct model shows how each team performs, assuming six person-hours of labor.

The conclusion is that the economist's production function is incorrect. It is an illusion that sets the stage for the marginal product of labor theories. A closer look at the data shows it is also a "set deck". Notice how the marginal product of labor, (column 3 figure 16) decreases every time a member is added to the team. In reality, the physical layout of an assembly area will determine the optimum number of people to hire. Productivity is almost never maximized with one worker.

Labor	Output	Marginal Product of Labor	Value of the Marginal Product of Labor	Wage	Marginal Profit
L (number of workers)	Q (bushels per week)	$MPL = \Delta Q/\Delta L$ (bushels per week)	$VMPL = P \times MPL$	W	$\Delta Profit = VMPL - W$
0	0				
		100	$1,000	$500	$500
1	100				
		80	800	500	300
2	180				
		60	600	500	100
3	240				
		40	400	500	-100
4	280				
		20	200	500	-300
5	300				

Ch 5 Figure 21 – Mankiw's Marginal Product of Labor

Marginal Product of Labor

Mankiw continues the card trick by presenting similar data for apple pickers.[38] (See figure 21) Notice this is the same data as the cookies-per-hour example multiplied by two, which should make someone wonder if the data is made up. Mankiw justifies the data as follows:

"At first, when only a few workers are hired, they can pick the low-hanging fruit. As the number of workers increases, additional workers have to climb higher up the ladders to find apples to pick."

This statement does not reflect what actually happens at the apple orchard. The farmer will hire a crew of workers to pick all of the apples. If a worker picked only the low-hanging fruit, he would probably get fired or kicked out by his fellow workers. In reality, a team of workers will work a tree, with different roles assigned to the workers. Some may focus on the tops of

---

38 Ibid Page 378

(1)	(2)	(3)	(4)	(5)	(6)
				Person	
	Team		Weeks to	Weeks to	Cost at
Number	Productivity:	Productivity	Harvest	Harvest	$500 per
Of	Bushels per	Bushels per	300	300	person
Worlers	week	Man Week	Bushells	Bushels	week
1	100	100	3	3.00	$ 1,500
2	180	90	1.67	3.33	$ 1,667
3	240	80	1.25	3.75	$ 1,875
4	280	70	1.07	4.29	$ 2,143
5	300	60	1.00	5.00	$ 2,500

Ch 5 Figure 22 – Productivity Table

the trees, with proper equipment such as ladders or lifts, while others will focus on lower fruit using picking tools mounted on poles. Others on the team will move the picked product to a collection point.

Mankiw finishes the card trick by claiming that the hiring will stop after three workers because the marginal profit is negative for the fourth or fifth worker. (See circle in figure 21).

Revealing Reality

The data for the apple pickers is similar to the cookie production example, and needs to be properly evaluated. The data is revised and shown in a productivity table. (See figure 22)

1. Column two is "Bushels per week". This is not a measure of output, but a rate that depends upon the size of the team. This column is re-labeled "Team productivity: Bushels per week".

2. Column three is a new value labeled "Productivity: Bushels per man-week." (Value = Column two / Column one)

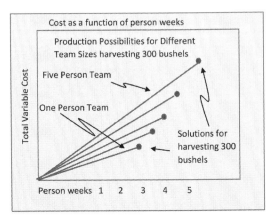

Ch 5 Figure 23 – Cost Functions by Team Size

3. Column four is "Weeks to Harvest 300 Bushels". This allows the manager to understand how time constraints would affect his/her choice of team size. (Value = 300 Bushels / Column 2)

4. Column five is "Person Weeks to Harvest 300 Bushels", a measure of labor-time required to harvest 300 bushels. (Value = 300 / Column 3)

5. Column six is cost to harvest, using the different team sizes. (Value = $500 x Colum 5)

Number of workers is not a sequentially dependent value. The farmer can hire any size team he wants. Consider a farmer who needs to harvest 300 bushels of apples. He has a choice of hiring a team of either 1, 2, 3, 4 or 5 workers. If he needs the apples harvested in one week, he has only one choice, a five-person team. If he is in no hurry, he could hire one worker and get the job done in three weeks. A graph of his options is shown below. (See figure 23)

The economist determined that three workers was the optimum solution. In reality, the least expensive approach is hiring just one worker. The respective cost per bushel would be either $1500/300 bushels for a cost of $5.00 a bushel for a one-person team or $2500/300 bushels for a cost of $8.33 per bushel for a five-person team. The team with the highest productivity will always be the team with the lowest cost.

Conclusions:

1. Marginal product of labor is a misapplied concept. Productivity is the proper concept to use when examining labor effectiveness. Given that the productivity of various-sized teams is usually determined by the physical layout of the production space, the number of workers is determined by the needs of the production space. Additional workers will only be hired when a new full-production shift needs to be added to the manufacturing process.

2. Economists teach that the labor demand curve is determined by the value of the marginal product curve.

    "As a result, the value-of-marginal-product curve is the labor-demand curve for a competitive profit maximizing firm."[39]

    Given that Mankiw's solution was incorrect; this theory can be thrown out.

---

39 Gregory Mankiw, *Economics* sixth edition, page 380, McGraw Hill, 2012

Given Mankiw's mistakes, there is no scientific justification for the concept of a demand curve for labor, based upon marginal product. Without supply and demand curves, the chartist theories that teach that a minimum wage, or unions, cause unemployment should be discarded. Raising wages can reduce profit margin, however, the impact on how many people are hired depends upon other factors.

Marginal Revenue; Card Trick #3

"It is the unspoken ethic of all magicians to not reveal their secrets."—David Copperfield

Economists promote the idea that firms in competitive markets earn no profits. However, most Americans are aware that firms with a monopoly clearly earn profits. To address this cognitive dissonance, economists craft a card trick called marginal revenue. Marginal revenue has the peculiar property that results in firms receiving less than the price paid by a customer. It is hard to imagine a customer paying $10 for an item while the firm only receives $7. This is exactly what economists teach.

Marginal Revenue

It is helpful to visit an accountant's view of a typical business process for recording revenue before exploring the card trick used by economists. Consider the following table, that demonstrates the simple relationship between the three elements, quantity, price, and total revenue. (See figure 24)

The economist takes this same table and creates a new table. At first pass, the table seems the same as an accountant's. (See figure 25) However, there are several significant changes that need explanation.

Quantity	Price	Total Revenue
1	$ 6.00	$ 6.00
2	$ 6.00	$ 12.00
3	$ 6.00	$ 18.00
4	$ 6.00	$ 24.00
5	$ 6.00	$ 30.00
6	$ 6.00	$ 36.00
7	$ 6.00	$ 42.00
8	$ 6.00	$ 48.00

Ch 5 Figure 24 – Accountant's View

Quantity (Q)	Price (P)	Total Revenue (TR = P x Q)	Marginal Revenue (MR = ΔTR/ΔQ)
0	$ 11	$ –	
			$ 10
1	$ 10	$ 10	
			$ 8
2	$ 9	$ 18	
			$ 6
3	$ 8	$ 24	
			$ 4
4	$ 7	$ 28	
			$ 2
5	$ 6	$ 30	
			$ –
6	$ 5	$ 30	
			$ (2)
7	$ 4	$ 28	
			$ (4)
8	$ 3	$ 24	

Ch 5 Figure 25 – Economist's View

1.   Price varies from one item to the next.

Anyone who has worked a cash register knows that the second pair of socks is priced the same as the first pair of socks. The economist provides the following explanation:

> "If the monopolist produces 1 gallon of water, it can sell that gallon for $10. If it produces 2 gallons of water, it must lower the price to $9 to sell both gallons."[40]

Without telling anyone, the definition for column one has changed. It no longer stands for the first, second, and third item sold, but now represents a total quantity to be sold during a "demand" period. Column one is now a rate of sales not a quantity of sales.

The last column, labeled marginal revenue, no longer fits the economist's own definition:

> "Marginal Revenue: the change in total revenue from an additional unit sold."

The last column now represents the difference in total revenue for selling a batch of gallons. A three-gallon batch has a total revenue of $24 and a four-gallon batch has a total revenue of $28, for a difference of $4. The card trick is complete. Most students and teachers will shake their heads and wonder about the new math discovered by economists. All sense of understanding is shrouded in mystery, as Marginal Revenue becomes something it is not.

With some encouragement, a high school student can

---

40 Gregory Mankiw, *Economics* sixth edition, page 282, McGraw Hill, 2012

prepare a simple argument against an economist's new math. If column 1 is for a rate of production, and the price is $8 when 3 units per demand cycle are being sold, wouldn't the revenue be

$$Total\ Revenue = \$8 + \$8 + \$8 = \$24$$

Each item sold results in $8 of revenue. By definition, the additional revenue for an additional unit sold is $8. Marginal Revenue is not the not the $6 shown in the table.

The student has been fooled to believe there is a new conceptual item, Marginal Revenue, which is not the same as price, and which causes firms to collect less than the going price!

Conclusion:

1. Price is always marginal revenue.

2. The model for monopoly is incorrect.

Marginalism Conclusion:

Francis Bacon warned about scientist drawing conclusions that do not exist . . .

> "The human understanding is, of its own nature, prone to suppose the existence of more order and regularity in the world than it finds."[41]

Economists were so strongly drawn to their conclusions, that they made up their own rules for mathematics to justify their ideas.

---

41   Francis Bacon, Novum Organum, 1620, XLV

1. Marginalism is based upon false mathematics.

2. Economic theories built upon marginalism have no mathematical justification.

3. Supply and demand curves do not exist.

Unlike the natural sciences which found mathematics reflected in nature's ballet, economists are plagiarizing Tchaikovsky while economics dances the jitterbug.

CHAPTER 6

Economic Smokescreens

Something intended to disguise, conceal, or deceive.

THIS CHAPTER WILL be new territory for readers that have not taken an economics class. Students and teachers will be very familiar with the terms and concepts, and should be entertained by a new perspective on these old ideas. Without the smoke and mirrors, a new understanding is possible.

1. Circular Flow

2. Opportunity Costs

3. Return on Investment

The Nature of Money

One of the most difficult concepts to grasp in economics is the dual nature of money. Money has value when it is sitting still and a different type of value when in motion. Paul Samuelson acknowledges this difference in his 1948 first edition:[42]

---

42 Paul Samuelson, *Economics*, First Edition, McGraw Hill, 1948 page 45

"Capital would be revealed by a still picture."

"Income, on the other hand, is by its nature a flow over time"

"Capital and Income are dimensionally incommensurable"

This concept is further complicated as certain flows feed into static pools, yet carry the same name. Savings can be the amount of money directed to savings during a time period or can refer to the total amount of value in the static account. This can be extremely confusing for the novice, but is handled routinely by businesses on a regular basis, using two standard financial reports:

Income Statement—A company's report covering a specified time frame for all monetary amounts that moved through the business, showing revenues, expenses, and resulting profit.

Balance Sheet—A company's report on static financial condition at a given time including three items. Assets are items of positive value owned by the firm. (Cash, equipment, etc.,) Liabilities are items of negative value such as debt. The final item in the balance sheet, net worth, is the difference between assets and liabilities.

In an economics class, very little time is spent learning these valuable reports and how they operate. This is unfortunate, as consumers who have been trained about these reports are better able to understand economics and personal finance. The critical idea of net worth comes directly from a balance sheet. The measures a bank uses to determine loan qualifications are based upon net worth and disposable income. Students are never taught about discretionary income, how to determine discretionary income and how it affects a personal budget. Why students are not taught this essential concept is a mystery. The impact is students have no idea about discretionary income and how that affects credit worthiness.

With an understanding of a balance sheet and an income statement, the reader is now prepared to critically view one of the first models introduced by an economist.

Our First Model: The Circular Flow Model

The idea for the circular flow model has its origin in *Tableau Economique,* published in 1758 by Frances Quesnay. There are many versions of the circular flow model today. The following model comes from Gregory Mankiw[43]. (See figure 1)

Mankiw claims:

"The diagram is a schematic representation of the organization of the economy."

All circular flow models used by economists are consistent in that they only recognize money in motion. There is little, if any, reference to static pools of money. If we look closely at Mankiw's diagram, we can spot an error as he refers to profits and shows profits being spent on factors of production, which is incorrect. Profits are not used to purchase factors of production, an amount referred to as working capital is used to purchase factors of production.

---

43   Gregory Mankiw, Principles of Economics Sixth Edition, 2012, South-Western Cengage Learning, Page 25

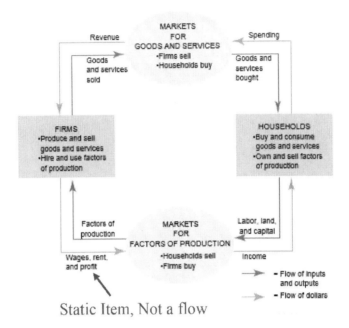

Static Item, Not a flow

Ch 6 Figure 1 – Circular Flow

Fixing Circular Flow

To fix this model, two things must be added,

1. A pool for static business assets, such as profits

2. A pool for static consumer assets, such as savings

Both of these additions are measures of static economic value that would be found on a balance sheet. These two changes significantly increase the usefulness of the model. The addition of static values reveals why people and firms participate in the economy. (See figure 2)

1. To have funds to cover operational or living costs.

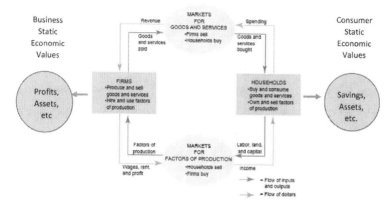

Ch 6 Figure 2 – Circular Flow Repaired

2. To improve their livelihood through accumulation
    of economic value.

The model opens the door to probing questions, such as
minimum wage laws. The model shows that with higher wages,
there will be an increase in GDP related to wages, which will
increase consumer spending and possibly consumer savings.
This same increase in minimum wage will reduce profits for
the firm. If profits are jeopardized, the livelihood of the firm
could be at risk. Profits must exist or the flow comes to a stop.
With larger profits, there is less of a guarantee the money will be
spent immediately as it could simply sit in the bank.

Conclusion:

Economic education must inform people about the dual
nature of money. The circular flow model is worthless without
a reference to balance sheet items. Economics classes should
be replaced with financial literacy, where students learn about
income statements, profits, balance sheets, and net worth.

Opportunity Cost

Magicians use a variety of techniques in performing magic.
One technique is referred to as mental forcing. Mental forcing
is where a magician effectively rewrites a spectator's vague
memory of a selected concept. In this case, the economist will
force a type of cost into an arena where it does not belong.

Economists teach that there are no profits for competitive
firms in competitive markets. In reality, profits must exist for
economic systems to operate. Economists are hiding profits to
avoid the discussion of how much profit is enough and how
much of the profit stream should be shared with workers.

In order to explain how a business continues to operate
when there are no profits, the economist misapplies the concept
of opportunity costs.

Origin of Opportunity Cost

Benjamin Franklin is often credited with one of the earliest
references to the concept of opportunity cost:

> "Remember that time is money. He that can earn ten
> shillings a day by his labour, and goes abroad, or sits idle
> one half of that Day, tho' he spends but Sixpence during
> his diversion or idleness, ought not to reckon that the only
> expence is sixpence; he has really spent or rather thrown
> away five shillings besides."[44]

Ben's famous "Time is Money" parable is about opportunity
cost, the idea that a person's cost should include any direct

---

44   Benjamin Franklin, *Advice to a Young Tradesman*, 1748

expenditures plus any foregone opportunity. Thus, opportunity costs is the sum of the two, as both were sacrificed.

It is important to clarify the context of opportunity cost. This is a situation where a person is considering a decision or examining the impact of a decision. If someone is considering the action of taking a half day off work, and spending money, the total cost is the expenditure and the foregone earnings. Any opportunity cost discussion must involve the context of choice.

An Economist's Explanation of Opportunity Cost

The economist goes to great lengths to explain how a concept related to a choice can be applied to day to day operations of running a business and determining profitability. The goal is achieved by using concepts that are unfamiliar to the student and by creating a new term, "economic profits," which are not the same as "accounting profits". Three types of cost are used to substantiate the idea of economic profits:

1. Opportunity Costs: Whatever must be given up to obtain some item.[45]

2. Explicit Costs: input costs that require an outlay of money by the firm.

3. Implicit Costs: input costs that do not require an outlay of money by the firm.

Mankiw explains his thoughts with a diagram and description of how accountants and economists measure profit differently. (See figure 3)

---

45 Mankiw, Glossary page 836

Accounting vs. Economics

Ch 6 Figure 3

"Figure 3 summarizes this difference. Notice that because the accountant ignores implicit costs, accounting profit is usually larger than economic profit".[46]

Unfortunately, this statement is not true. Accountants deal with implicit costs all the time. Some simple, but major, examples include:

1. Depreciation
2. Inventory consumption
3. Asset depletion

Any time an accountant moves something from the balance sheet to the income statement, the process is accommodated using implicit costs. For this comparison to be realistic, the model must show accounting implicit costs and economic implicit costs. (See figure 4)

---

46   Ibid page 262

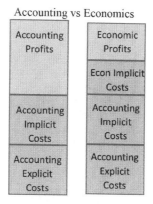

Ch 6 Figure 4 – Adding Implicit Costs

From the corrected diagrams, the relationship between accounting and economic profits becomes . . .

Accounting Profits – Economic Implicit Costs = Economic Profits

Mankiw provides guidance on economic implicit costs with the following sentence:

"For every hour that Caroline works at her cookie factory, she gives up $100 income she could have earned as a programmer, and this forgone income is also part of her cost."[47]

What about context?

The economist has the student so busy thinking about things they don't understand, that they fail to recall that opportunity

---

47   Ibid page 261

costs require the context of choice. If Caroline has a decision to make, yes, she should compare her salary as a programmer to her profits in her business to make the decision. This does not eliminate her profits at the cookie factory. Maybe the programmer position has been filled? Opportunity cost is a point in time comparison. It is not an on-going factor that determines profitability.

Mental Forcing

The word cost is tightly coupled with running a business. Once a person encounters the word cost, the idea of giving up money or something of value comes to mind. It is very easy to push the idea of opportunity cost into the framework of running a business, but it is incorrect to conclude that opportunity cost affects day-to-day profitability. The instructor's authority and trust, given to him by virtue of his position, is exploited in order to confuse the student. Likewise, the trust extended to the author and publisher of the economics books has the same effect upon the high school economics teacher. The end result is the student is confused about profits.

To see how absurd this concept is, in the eyes of the economists, it is possible to argue that Bill Gates did not have any economic profits while working at Microsoft. Mr. Gates had other opportunities to consider. He could have been just as successful starting up Gatesoft instead. Assuming he "gave up" the profits from Gatesoft, he would have no economic profits at Microsoft.

Trying to Apply the Opportunity Cost Concept

Mankiw does not stop there, but continues to distort the issue with an example dealing with financing a business. Mankiw presents a situation where Caroline's cookie business has a choice about how to finance the business.[48] For option A, Caroline provides $300,000 of her own money to run the business and in option B Caroline borrows $200,000s and provides $100,000 of her own money. Given this involves a choice, one might expect opportunity cost to work, but it fails miserably.

Mankiw explains that the cost of Caroline's capital should include an opportunity cost, and suggests that accountants are making mistakes when ignoring foregone interest as an implicit opportunity cost.

Option A—Self-Financed business with $300,000 personal investment.

Option B—Borrowed $200,000 and provided $100,000 to start and run the same business.

Assuming the business had a profit of $50k prior to interest expense, and interest rates were 5%, the following income statements could be derived by an accountant or an economist. (See figure 5)

The following instructions from Mankiw explain option B, with $200,000 financing.

"Caroline's accountant, who only measures explicit costs, will now count the $10,000 (See #1 above) interest toward the cost ... By contrast, according to an economist, the opportunity cost of owning the business is still $15,000. The opportunity cost equals the interest on the bank loan ($10,000) plus the forgone interest on savings ($5,000) (See #2 above)

---

48 Gregory Mankiw, *Principles of Economics* Sixth Edition, Cengage Learning, 2012 page 261

Accountants View "Without Opportunity Costs"		
	Option A	Option B
Carolines Cookies	No Financing	$200,000 Financing
Profit before Interest	$ 50,000.00	$ 50,000.00
		#1
Interest Expense	$ -	$ 10,000.00
Net Profit	$ 50,000.00	$ 40,000.00

Economists View "With Opportunity Costs"		
	Option A	Option B
Carolines		$200,000
Cookies	No finacing	Financing
Profit before Interest	$ 50,000.00	$ 50,000.00
Interest Expense	$ -	$ 10,000.00
		#2
Opportunity Cost	$ 15,000.00	$ 5,000.00
Economic Profit	$ 35,000.00	$ 35,000.00

Ch 6 Figure 5 – Financing Decision:
With and without Opportunity Costs

In the case of the economist, the economic profit is EXACTLY the same for the two financing alternatives, $35,000, making it impossible to make a decision.

In the case of the accountant, the profit for the two alternatives are either $50,000 self-financed or $40,000 with a $200,000 loan. The irony is that by applying the economist's idea of opportunity costs, Caroline is not able to choose between self-financing $300,000 or borrowing $200,000. If Caroline sticks with her accountant, she can clearly see the effect of financing her acquisition, profits will be reduced by the amount of interest expense.

Mankiw concludes the discussion with the following sentence:

"To understand business decisions, we need to keep an eye on economic profit."[49]

---

49   Ibid page 262

Opportunity costs and economic profits don't make sense when discussing profitability.

Conclusion:

1. Opportunity Cost is a simple way to compare choices. Opportunity Costs have no relationship to actual profits. Financial analysis using present value is the preferred method for assessing choices in business. No one in the real world uses opportunity costs to measure ongoing profitability.

2. Economists confuse the student by claiming that Opportunity Cost is an implicit cost when, in fact, it is not a cost at all. It is a value trade-off between two different choices.

3. Economists confuse the student further by claiming accountants do not address implicit costs. In reality, accountants must address implicit costs all the time.

Return on Investment Vs Diminishing Returns

"Grand theory is drunk on syntax, blind to semantics. Its practitioners do not truly understand that, when we define a word, we are merely inviting others to use it as we would like it to be used; that the purpose of definition is to focus argument upon fact and that the proper result of good definitions to transform argument over terms into disagreements about fact, and thus open argument to further inquiry."[50] C. Wright Mills

---

50 C. Wright Mills, *The Sociological Imagination*, Oxford University Press, 2000, page 34

In the mind of C. Wright Mills, economics would qualify as a grand theory which focuses on highly abstract concepts with little relation to the real world. The departure from reality and facts becomes apparent when words assume new and different meanings. One of those words in the world of economics is the word return.

In the world of finance, return is a measure of profitability. Specifically -

$$Return\ on\ Investment = ROI = \frac{Profits\ made\ in\ a\ year}{amount\ of\ money\ invested}$$

Economic History and Return in Farming

Unfortunately, over the years, economists have often used return as a measure of productivity. The root of the confusion comes from the early economists when they were analyzing profitability of farms in the 1800's. Consider a farmer who owned three 100-acre parcels of land. Each of these parcels had different levels of productivity, which tied directly to levels of profit. (See figure 6)

As the farmer employs less productive land, the harvest derives fewer bushels per acre. Assuming the cost of the acre is constant, the rate of return diminishes with diminishing productivity. In the case of a farm, return and productivity are directly related when the capital cost of the additional land is factored into the calculations. From this model, economist eventually developed an improper view of diminishing return.

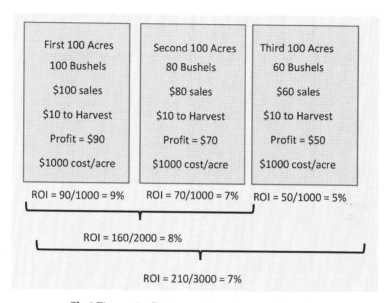

Ch 6 Figure 6 – Return on Investment—Farming

Diminishing Returns *The property whereby the benefit from an extra unit of input declines as the quantity of input increases.*[51]

In the example using the farm, diminishing profits/returns are directly associated with diminishing productivity. However, this is not the case with labor.

Measuring Return with Labor

In the case of labor, the value of return is not affected in the same way. Consider a manufacturer who has the option of

---

51   Gregory Mankiw, *Principles of Economics* sixth edition page 541

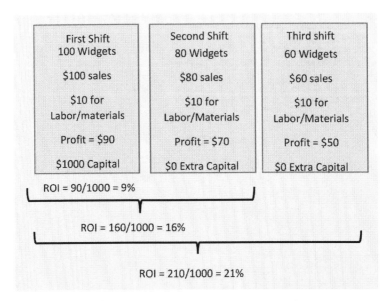

Ch 6 Figure 7 – Return on Investment—Manufacturing

running additional shifts. Even if productivity decreases, ROI will increase. The key observation is that the impact on return is more complicated when considering inputs, such as labor, that do not require additional invested capital. In the case where labor is the additional input, and capital is constant, adding an input of labor that is less effective does not cause return on investment to go down. (See figure 7)

For this reason, the economist's definition of diminishing returns should be recognized as a measure of productivity, not a measure of return.

Consider an auto factory. An extra unit of input could be man-hours, and the quantity produced would be cars. Diminishing returns would predict less relative output for extra input.

$$Diminishing\ Return = \frac{fewer\ Cars\ produced}{with\ more\ Man\text{-}hours}$$

This same term for someone managing a factory would be called productivity.

$$Productivity = \frac{Cars\ produced}{Man\text{-}hours}$$

When productivity goes down, there are fewer cars produced for each man-hour consumed. This situation would definitely increase the cost of production. However, without knowing actual quantities sold, prices, total revenue, and other cost factors, profit and return cannot be determined.

Economist are confusing students with out of date terminology. The term "Diminishing Returns" needs to focus on profitability, not productivity.

Conclusion:

An economics course includes several concepts that are traditional ideas that do not hold up to close inspection.

1. Circular flow fails to recognize the difference between static and dynamic measures of economic systems. Adding income statements and balance sheets would significantly improve the students' understanding of economic systems.

2. Opportunity costs do not affect real profits. Teaching this concept confuses the students.

3. Return on investment is about profits. Economists are stuck on concepts from the 1800's that fail to

understand the basic math involved in computing return. They fail to recognize the difference between productivity and profitability.

4. Economics fails to teach students the concept of discretionary income and how it affects credit worthiness or personal budgeting.

CHAPTER 7

Replacing Supply and Demand Curves

"There is much evidence showing that, once an uncertain situation has been perceived or interpreted in a particular fashion, it is quite difficult to view it in any other way" Danny Kahneman *(Nobel prize winner in Economics, 2002) and Amos Tversky*

WHILE WRITING THIS book, the invariable question was typically: "If there are no supply and demand curves, what is there?" There is a completely different and more realistic way to view product markets. The following four steps pave the way for the reader to see markets in a new light.

1. A closer look reveals different laws

2. Walk in the shoes of two economists that came close

3. Law of Supply rethought

4. New view of a market

Closer Look

Using the proper form of a conditional statement, the laws of supply and demand can be written more clearly.

Law of Demand: If all else is equal, when the price rises, the quantity demanded falls.

Corollary: When prices fall, the quantity demanded increases

Law of Supply: If all else is equal, when the price rises, the quantity supplied rises.

Corollary: When prices fall, the quantity supplied decreases.

Notice both laws have the same condition, all else equal. If everything is equal all the time due to ceteris paribus, this means both laws apply all the time. Notice the laws predict exactly opposite results even though they have the same pre-condition of all else is equal. When the price rises, the Law of Demand predicts quantity decreases and the Law of Supply predicts quantities will increase. How does an economist determine which law should be in effect and what is the predicted result for quantity sold? Recall, one of the basic premises for a scientific law is to provide a prediction or explain subsequent phenomenon. The laws of supply and demand fail to explain anything.

By slightly changing the perspective, one can see the laws are trying to describe what occurs in the case of surplus or scarcity. This leads to a different set of laws:

First Law of Surplus: If there is a surplus, quantities produced will tend to decline.

Second Law of Surplus: If there is a surplus, merchants will tend to reduce their prices to increase the rate of consumption and eliminate the surplus.

First Law of Shortage: If there is a shortage, quantities produced will tend to increase.

Second Law of Shortage: If there is a shortage, merchants will tend to increase prices to increase profits and slow consumption until the shortage is eliminated.

These laws provide a clear description of how merchants and consumers will respond to differing situations in a market, and they apply all the time, given the pre-conditions of surplus or scarcity. These laws eliminate any ambiguity inherent in the laws of supply and demand. Not only do these laws stand up to the test of common sense, examples are easy to identify. When the realtor says it is a buyer's market, it is a direct result of a perceived surplus of houses for sale. When the realtor says it is a seller's market, it is a direct result of a perceived shortage of houses for sale. Buyer's markets will tend to have lower prices and seller's markets will tend to have higher prices.

Recall in Chapter 4, there were six factors identified that affect price:

1. Choice
2. Perceived level of need
3. Knowledge
4. Time
5. Personal Power
6. Variations in flow

The sixth factor, variations in flow, captures the impact of surplus and scarcity.

The conclusion is supply and demand curves are poor proxies for modeling market behavior.

Walking in the Shoes of H.L. Moore, Statistical Economics, circa 1910

Earlier in Chapter 3, the story of H. L. Moore was introduced. Moore was an early economist who did not believe in supply and demand curves. He believed statistics could be used to validate economic theories; however, his studies raised questions that could not be answered by theories based upon supply and demand curves. In his paper, "Economic Cycles", Moore reported finding demand curves that sloped upwards and downwards:.

> "In the one case, as the product increases or decreases, the price falls or rises; while, in the other case, the price rises with an increase of the product and falls with its decrease."[52]

To propose that demand curves could be upward or downward sloping was to suspend belief in Alfred Marshall's supply and demand curves. E J Working wrote a critical article on Moore's work, claiming that his upward-sloping demand curve had been misunderstood. Working asked this question about H. L. Moore's statistical analysis:

---

52   HL Moore, Economic Cycles, Their Law and Cause, New York, The Macmillan Company, 1914, page 114

"Is it not evident that Professor Moore's "Laws of Demand" for pig iron is in reality a "Law of Supply" instead?"[53]

The economics profession was not interested in addressing Moore's conflicting data, and willingly accepted Working's conclusion that Moore was confused. However, a brief historical perspective sheds light on Working and Moore's confusion.

Pig Iron

In western Kentucky, there is a wonderful National Recreation Area called *The Land Between the Lakes*. In the area, there are historical ruins of pig iron furnaces, with descriptions of the key economic role these furnaces played in the local economy. Step one in the iron industry was the gathering of iron ore, typically hematite, from the local hills and melting the ore in a large brick furnace. The melted iron would pour out of the furnace into channels prepared in wet sand. A center channel would carry the main flow which branched into smaller channels. The main channel was called the sow and the smaller channels were the pigs, thus the term pig iron.

Pig iron by itself is not of much use and must be refined once again before it becomes an input for products made of steel or cast iron.

This was the market H. L. Moore was studying. Moore was examining the market from the view of the second stage processor who was buying pig iron. Moore was collecting statistics on prices paid and quantities purchased. From this

53   E J Working, What Do Statistical Demand Curve Show? Readings in Price Theory, page 105, The American Economic Association Series, Ruskin House, 1953

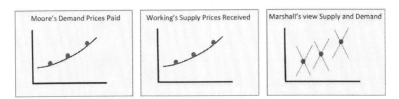

Ch 7 Figure 1 – Moore, Working and Marshall Ponder the data

data, Moore discovered the demand curves that sloped either upward or downward.

Working claimed Moore was confused and was actually seeing supply curves. In retrospect, they were both correct, and they were both confused. Moore's data for demand, the prices and quantities purchased, is exactly the same as the data for supply, the prices and quantities sold. Moore saw demand curves, and Working saw supply curves. These two sets of data will always match. (See figure 1)

If Alfred Marshall had been willing to comment on Moore's work, he would have provided the third chart, showing supply and demand curves moving to new positions. However, that would have been the end of the laws of supply and demand, for two reasons:

1. Nothing stayed the same—supply curves and demand curves had to move in order for prices to have changed. There is no such thing as static equilibrium.

2. Most importantly, Marshall's diagram reveals that it is impossible to observe a supply curve or a demand curve, only the intersection, or the data related to an actual sale, is ever revealed. There is no data to collect that could represent a supply or demand curve.

Perhaps this is why Marshall avoided Moore.

Francis Bacon would conclude there is no scientific justification for supply and demand curves, as there are no observations. Scientists only deal with observable phenomenon. The only conclusion a scientist would reach is time has come to return to step one and propose a better idea.

Rethinking the Law of Supply

Mankiw provides a supply curve as shown,[54] with the companion law of supply: (See figure 2)

The claim that other things equal, the quantity supplied of a good rises when the price of the good rises.

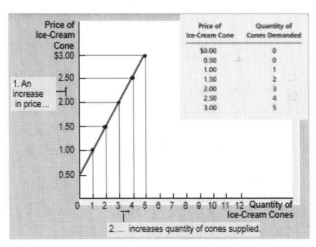

Ch 7 Figure 2 – Mankiw's Supply Curve

---

54 Gregory Mankiw, page 74

Even if this claim is true sometimes, it does not describe the behavior of a supplier. It would be valuable to incorporate two common-sense rules:

1. A supplier cannot sustain production if the price is below cost.

2. A supplier can sell one item for a profit at a given price. The supplier can increase profits by selling more items at the same price.

These common-sense rules make it clear that there is a minimum price in a market, which is cost. The characteristics of the product and market will determine how much the price elevates above cost. Selling more at the same price is very likely to happen and would predict a flat supply curve.

If there is a flat supply curve, what will the price be?

Price Determination

A new method that examines the interaction of supplier and consumer clarifies how a price range is established. Consider two breakeven models that show product profitability for two different firms. (See figure 3)

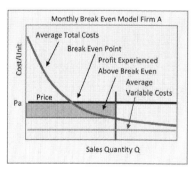
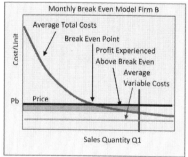

Ch 7 Figure 3 – Breakeven for two firms

The shaded area on the graph represents profits based upon total sales for a given month, price of the product, and average total costs. Assuming similar firms with similar products, the charts show that firm B has a lower price. If one determines consumer choice solely on price competition, firm B will have higher monthly sales. The lower price may or may not allow for increased profits. Profits will be dependent upon the cost structure of the firm and how much market share Firm B is able to capture. Note that firm A could increase profits by raising its price, assuming quantity sold does not change. However, with similar products, a price increase could result in decreased sales and a possible decrease in profits. No firm can sustain operations when the best price they can earn is below their cost.

The supplier's dynamic trade-off between more sales at a lower price and fewer sales at a higher price creates the pressure on net profits, resulting in prices that fluctuate above cost but below a price that stimulates price-based competition for market share.

Improved View of Competitive Market

Consider the following view of how a market is served. (see figure 4) In a competitive market, there are many suppliers with similar products and similar prices. Consumers can choose between the various providers, based upon price, quality, or features incorporated into the product. The total quantity consumed is variable, rising and falling with the life breath of society. The model demonstrates three realistic features:

1. Profits for suppliers
2. Varying quantities, based upon economic activity or market share gains/losses.

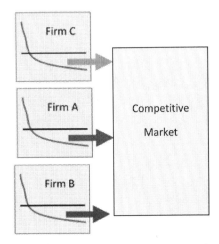

Ch 7 Figure 4 – Many firms—one Market

3. Multiple prices available for products, with differing features in those products to assist in gaining market share.

The break-even model demonstrates how different providers can have different cost structures, based upon sales volume. (See figure 5) The dots represent two operating levels for different firms. The higher the quantity sold, the lower average total costs, the higher the profit margin, and the higher total profit.

The supply from a single competitor has two primary data points, price and average total costs. A market with several providers would have several prices, matched with different costs. If providers cannot make a profit, they will leave the market. The surviving providers must manage costs and must price-position their product, given the other players in the market.

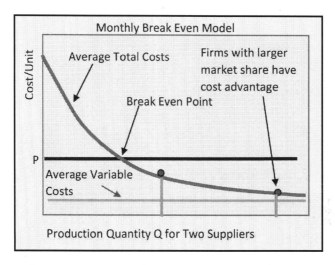

Ch 7 Figure 5 – Cost advantage with larger market share

The cumulative market supply appears as multiple supplier prices and multiple supplier costs. The potential for profit is the difference between price and cost. (See figure 6)

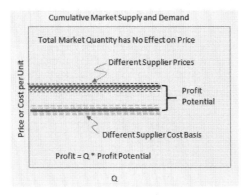

Ch 7 Figure 6 – Flat supply and demand?

Key checks with reality:

1. Profits are included in the model.

2. Actual costs experienced by each supplier will vary, based upon their volume of output and cost structure.

3. Profits are maximized by selling as many items as possible, managing costs, and competing with product features to prevent price erosion.

4. Price can be used to attract more sales. However, the effectiveness of expanding profits will depend upon prices available from competitors and the provider's average total cost. Other tactics for expanding sales may be more effective.

Perhaps the most important observation is that, with the flat line for cost and price, there is no relationship between price of a good and quantity supplied. It is common sense that, if a supplier can provide one product at a given price, more profits will be available by selling additional items. A price increase is not required to motivate the provider to sell another item. There is no upward sloping supply curve.

Tempting Conclusion

It is very tempting to conclude that price is a flat demand curve and that cost is a flat supply curve. However, now is the time to jump out of the box and ask two questions:

What is supply? What is demand? Supply and demand are two sides of a trade.

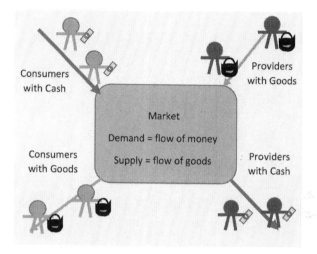

Ch 7 Figure 7 – Two sides of the same coin

Supply—The flow of economic value in the form of goods from a manufacturer/provider to a buyer/consumer. Measured in quantity of goods or revenue.

Demand—The flow of economic value in the form of money from the buyer/consumer to a manufacturer/provider. Measured in money. (See figure 7)

Price can vary with each and every transaction.

The goal of the consumer is to pay as little as possible. The goal of the provider is to receive as much as possible. There are factors that determine price; however, they are not solely based upon quantity supplied and/or quantity demanded.

Markets

Economists today teach that all markets are driven by the sterile interaction of quantity and price, with the hallowed supply and demand curve determining all outcomes, regardless of the type of market. This is inaccurate. A quick scan reveals three different markets that are driven by wildly different factors.

1. Product market—Purchases of products are independent random events. Sustainable markets will have a minimum price of just above cost and maximum price as high as anyone will pay.

2. Labor Market—Purchases of labor are a combination of time and effort—person hours. Labor wages associated with production are typically paid hourly. Inspection and direction wages are typically paid over a longer period and are salaried wages. Economics treats labor as just another input for economic activity, failing to identify the difference between a lump of coal and a fellow citizen.

3. Financial Markets—These markets represent exchanges of financial assets. There is no production cost or profit as experienced in the markets for goods. There is no time consumed as there is no work required once the asset is acqured. The price for a financial asset floats in the minds of the speculator, similar to how beauty is assessed differently by various observers.

In Chapter 4, six factors that drive the product market were identified. Each factor either favors the buyer or the provider.

Instead of using a supply and demand curve, which is as useful as a yin and yang symbol, a better symbol for a market for products would be:

Seller's Market	Buyer's Market
1. Choices restricted in some manner	1. Many choices, products, providers
2. Must Have Items, High Perceived Needs, High Emotional Sentiment	2. Low perceived need, purchase can be foregone
3. Knowledge, complex product	3. Knowledge: Familiar product
4. Time, perceived or real urgency to buy	4. Time, urgency to sell
5. Personal Assertiveness – influential sales staff	5. Personal Assertiveness – buyer who is willing to negotiate or shop
6. Variations in flow – high growth rate, shortage, fixed quantity	6. Variations in flow – low growth rate, surplus

Laws for Buyer's and Seller's Markets

Proposed laws for product markets might be:

1. **Law of Choice:** Buyer's markets are more likely when the consumer has more choices.

2. **Law of Needs and Wants:** Buyer's markets are less likely as a product moves from different stages of desire: awareness → want → need → must have. (Water is a great exception as society usually sees that water is provided at cost or with a very minimum level of profit. Water is a great example of a public good that is best provided without a profit motive.)

3. **Law of Knowledge:** Buyer's markets are less likely when a product is complex or difficult to understand. A consumer needs to be well-informed in order to know they are paying a fair price.

4. **Law of Time:** Markets are affected by time pressures on buyers and sellers. Consumers in a hurry will typically overpay. Merchants in a hurry will typically sell for less.

5. **Law of Personal Influence.** Buyer's markets are more likely when consumers have confidence to stand up for themselves and shop assertively. Seller's markets are more likely with high pressure sales staff pushing consumers to make decisions.

6. **Laws of surplus and shortage**

   a. **First Law of Surplus:** If there is a surplus, quantities produced will tend to decline.

   b. **Second Law of Surplus:** If there is a surplus, merchants will tend to reduce their prices to increase the rate of consumption and eliminate the surplus.

   c. **First Law of Shortage:** If there is a shortage, quantities produced will tend to increase.

   d. **Second Law of Shortage:** If there is a shortage, prices will tend to rise to slow consumption and increase profits per item until the shortage is eliminated.

These are laws that are easily taught and understood. They provide tremendous insight for young shoppers as they start their life as working adults.

The laws also show where regulations are required to make

markets fair. A large area for regulations deals with knowledge of complex products. The idea of requiring the disclosure of an "APR", Annual Percentage Rate, is to assure consumers can effectively compare loan products with differing ways of charging interest. The idea of making health insurance policies follow a set of various standards, is meant to allow consumers to make easy comparisons between complex products.

In the early 1900s, the anti-trust laws were meant to assure choice in the marketplace.

There are laws that protect consumers from time pressured salesmanship at their own front door. These laws are referred to as "FTC Cooling Off Rules",[55] which provide the consumer with three days to void the sale. The rule only applies to sales at your home, workplace, dormitory, convention center or restaurant. They are related to two market conditions noted above—Law of Time and Law of Personal Influence.

Conclusion:

What consumers truly want are fair markets. Free markets are ambiguous concepts tied to the idea of American Freedom. Americans see few free markets, as most markets have been influenced by corporations to create sellers markets. The Pharmaceutical market is a tremendous sellers' market, one of the most protected markets today by way of several techniques (patents, mergers to reduce choice, price fixing through legislation).

Consumers need to be aware of these six factors when entering a market in order to make informed decisions.

---

55   https://www.consumer.ftc.gov/articles/0176-buyers-remorse-when-ftcs-cooling-rule-may-help

1. Choice—Keep options open to create a buyers' market

2. Perceived need—Don't be fooled by clever advertising. Understand what meets your needs.

3. Knowledge—Shopping is how one learns about products before buying.

4. Time—Patience prevents excitement from overpaying.

5. Personal Assertiveness.—Only you can request a lower price.

6. Variations in flow/availability—Be aware of opportunities created by a surplus and hazards created by shortages.

The theory that counter-sloping supply and demand curves create equilibrium points for market prices fails to describe what actually happens in economics. Any further discussion about the economy should refrain from using chartist-based theories from Neoclassical Economists. It is safe to say that any related postulates from Neoclassical Economics can also be discarded. (See figure 8)

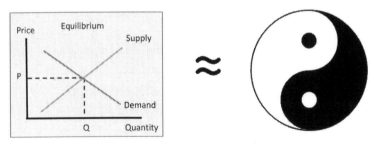

Ch 7 Figure 8 – Societal Symbols—
False Science of Supply and Demand vs Taoism Yin and Yang

The supply and demand curve has become a Braidism for western culture and will be difficult to replace. Very few symbols carry as much weight. It has, at times, been compared to the Chinese symbol of Yin and Yang. However, the Yin and Yang symbol of Taoism has never claimed to have science as its foundation. Someday, people might consider the parallels between the science of economics and the Donation of Constantine.

CHAPTER 8

Groupthink

"Groupthink refers to a deterioration of mental efficiency, reality testing, and moral judgment that results from in-group pressures."

—Irving Janis [56]

THE SCIENCE OF economics, which is not based on any scientific principles, became an ideology taught at all major universities and in most high schools across the US and the western world. Even though the curves have never been observed in life, they occupy a prime spot in the minds of most Americans. They provide an unstable foundation for society's understanding of how economic systems actually work.

The term Groupthink first appeared in a publication in 1971, where Irving Janis described situations involving decision-making that were severely compromised due to group behavioral dynamics. Eight symptoms were identified by Irving

---

56   Irving L. Janis, *Groupthink*, Houghton Mifflin, 1982, page 9

that are characteristic of Groupthink. Seven of these are useful for exploring the development of economic theory.

1. Sense of invulnerability
2. Moral justification
3. Rationalization
4. Stereotyping of outsiders
5. Pressure to conform
6. Self-censorship
7. Unanimity—Not important since a group decision is not required in this comparison.
8. Mindguards

Supportive articles, such as the article from Daniel B. Klein and Charlotta Stern, *Groupthink in Academia,* agree that groupthink is a behavioral pattern to be avoided. Their conclusion: "Although academia differs from the settings explored by groupthink theorists, it exhibits many of the same tendencies and failings."[57]

The article called out specific conditions found in academia that contribute to Groupthink:

"Decision Makers Constitute a Cohesive Group. The professional pyramid and departmental autonomy tend toward group cohesiveness.

---

57 Daniel B. Klein and Charlotta Stern—*Groupthink in Academia, Majoritarian Department Politics and the Professional Pyramid.* The Independent Review V 13 Spring 2009, page 12

Insulation of the Group. No one outside the pyramid is qualified to judge the group. Insiders safely ignore outside opinion.

Homogeneity of Members' Social Background and Ideology. Sorting and molding mechanisms produce ideological homogeneity, both throughout the pyramid and within the individual department."

Symptom #1 Sense of Invulnerability

Alfred Marshall was an incredible leader in the development of Neoclassical Economics. He was responsible for establishing one of the first economics departments at a major university, Cambridge. In 1890, he published his *Principles of Economics.* The Cambridge University website still lavishes praise on his book:

> "... his great *Principles of Economics,* in which he set out for the first time the geometric analysis of supply and demand, incorporating the systematic treatment of different time periods."[58]

Alfred Marshall was a powerful and well-respected scholar. He had worked in the economics field for over fifty years and was referred to as the patriarch of Neoclassical Economics. Keynes, a former student, described his preeminence in a memorial published in 1924:

"In his (Marshall's) inaugural address of 1885, he said: "Twelve years ago, England possessed perhaps the ablest

---

58   http://www.econ.cam.ac.uk/about/history/

set of economists that there have ever been in a country at one time. But one after another they have been taken from us Mill, Cairnes, Bagehot, Cliffe Leslie, Jevons, Newmarch, and Fawcett." There was no one left who could claim at that date to approach Marshall in stature." [59]

The grandness of Marshall's theory was compared to Isaac Newton:

"The equilibrium point of Demand and Supply was extended so as to discover a whole Copernican system by which all the elements of the economic universe are kept in their places"[60]

Keynes also referenced a local newspaper story that trumpeted Marshall's new beliefs about economics.

"It is a great thing," said the Pall Mall Gazette, *"to have a Professor at one of our old Universities devoting the work of his life to recasting the science of Political Economy as the Science of Social Perfectibility."* The New Political Economy had arrived, and the Old Political Economy, the dismal science, *"which treated the individual man as a purely selfish and acquisitive animal,"* had passed away.[61]

59 J M Keynes, Alfred Marshall 1842-1924, *The Economic Journal*, September 1924 page 344

60 Ibid page 350

61 Ibid page 349

These accolades highlight the level of praise that contributed to the sense of invulnerability brewing at Cambridge during this time. This feeling extends to today. From Klein/Stern:

"Academics feel that those outside the pyramid lack knowledge and credibility, and that those inside the pyramid would not dare to become renegades." [62]

Add to this the observation from Keynes regarding academia in 1888 and Marshall's influence:

". . . half the economic chairs in England are held by his pupils" [63]

There was no one to challenge the new theories, as all the experts were from the same club. Criticism from other philosophers such as Henry George, Major Douglas or Karl Marx, was either ignored, rationalized away, or dismissed as unscientific.

Today, this sense of invulnerability extends to professors at universities and teachers in local high schools. In the classroom, there will be no challenge. The instructor is infallible and immune from question.

Symptom #2 Moral Justification

The 1800s were a tumultuous time, as the industrial revolution changed society in many ways. Capitalism and the industrial revolution caused serious harm to society, including

---

62   Daniel B. Klein and Charlotta Stern *Groupthink in Academia*

63   J. M. Keynes, *Alfred Marshall*—page 366

poor working conditions, child labor, poor pay, and rapid consumption of resources. Marx published *The Communist Manifesto* in 1848, an event which was quickly followed by revolutions in much of Western Europe. Since the *Manifesto* predicted that socialism would eventually replace capitalism as the core economic mode of operation, fear of communism lingered.

Throughout the 1800s, labor struggled for fair pay, safe working conditions, affordable housing, and affordable goods at the company store. Many strikes resulted in the death of union workers. Books of the time shared the cause of these struggles with the world. From *Progress and Poverty*, published in 1879:

> "The unjust distribution of wealth stemming from this fundamental wrong is separating modern society into the very rich and the very poor. The continuous increase of rent is the price labor is forced to pay for the use of land. It strips the many of wealth they justly earn, and heaps it in the hands of a few who do nothing to earn it." [64]

Karl Marx and Friedrich Engels published a total of three volumes of *Das Kapital*. Their works continued to highlight the undesirable aspects of capitalism, and promoted communism as a preferred social model. Volume one came in 1867, while volumes two and three came after Marx had died. They were published in 1885 and 1894.

Capitalism needed a moral champion and found that cham-

---

64 Henry George, *Progress and Poverty*, 2009 Robert Schalkenbach *Foundation* page 187

pion in Alfred Marshal's economic theories. These theories are the seeds for today's Neoclassical Economics, which promote these ideas:

1. Economic science shows that price is the result of the natural forces of supply and demand in a market. (i.e., Adam Smith's invisible hand.) Price gouging is a symptom of the market, not a demonstration of greed.

2. Economic science shows that workers are paid a wage based upon the natural forces of the market, driven by their marginal product of labor. Starvation wages for some and king's wages for others are naturally driven by the market, and not a demonstration of greed.

3. Economic science shows that everyone's welfare is maximized with free markets. Income inequality is a result of the natural forces in the market, and not a sign of an underpaid labor class resulting from pursuit of self interest on the part of owners.

4. Economic science shows that there are no profits in competitive markets. Karl Marx and other progressives questioning inequality fail to understand neoclassical economic science.

Just as Newton's *Principia Mathematica* displaced religious ideas about the heavens, Alfred Marshall's *Principles of Economics* elevated economics to a science, beyond the reach of moral judgement or philosophical debate. Marshall framed capitalism as a science that would benefit all of the participants, in a manner that was consistent with natural laws.

"Each element of cost would be governed by natural laws, subject to some control from fixed custom."[65]

By promoting capitalism as a natural science, economists claimed the high ground of morality, teaching society how systems work, with no apparent bias towards the owner/capitalist or the laborer.

Further evidence of the perceived morality behind economic theories comes from J. B Clark and his publication in 1899:

"The natural law of wages gives a result that would satisfy his own requirement, as being desirable and morally justifiable."[66]

An observation from John Pullen, an economics professor for more than 40 years.

"J. B. Clark (1899) . . . arguing that distribution according to marginal productivities is not only economically correct, but also morally correct. . . . Some see it as the ultimate answer to . . . writers such as Karl Marx. Henry George and Major Douglas."[67]

Throughout the 1900s, communism continued to pose a threat to the western way of life. Economists and economic

---

65 Alfred Marshall, *Principles of Economics*, 8th edition, Macmillan and Co. Limited, 1920, page 214

66 J. B. Clark, *The Distribution of Wealth: A Theory of Wages, Interest and Profits,* Online Library of Liberty, Page 249.

67 John Pullen, *The Marginal Productive Theory of Distribution, A Critical History,* London:Routledge, 2010

textbooks continued to provide scientifically-founded moral guidance on how society should operate.

Symptom #3 Rationalization

In 1914, H. L. Moore challenged Marshal's theories when he published *Economic Cycles: Their Law and Cause.*

> "The dogma of the uniformity of the law of demand is an idol of the static state." [68]

Moore presented data from his research that showed demand curves that moved counter to the law of demand. Instead of sloping downward, the data showed the curves sloping upward. Marshall ignored Moore's work, and other economists followed along. Finally, in 1927, after Marshall's death, E. J. Working responded with his paper; *What do Statistical "Demand Curves" Show?* His introductory sentences follow:

> "Many questions of practical importance hinge upon the elasticity of demand and supply. The economist can answer them only in a vague and indefinite manner because he does not know the nature of the demand curve." [69]

It is inappropriate for a scientist to claim lack of knowledge about a topic while at the same time proposing grand theories

---

68 H. L. Moore, *Economic Cycles, Their Law and Cause*, page 113, Macmillon Company 1914

69 E J Working, "What do Statistical Demand Curves Show?" *The Quarterly Journal of Economics* 1927

that are dependent upon that knowledge. The result is an introduction to a long rationalization.

Another famous rationalization comes from Milton Friedman's *The Methodology of Positive Economics*:[70]

> "To be important, therefore, a hypothesis must be descriptively false in its assumptions: it takes the account of, and accounts for none of, the many other attendant circumstances, since its very success shows them to be irrelevant to the phenomena to be explained."

This is akin to Orwell's doublethink, "War is Peace". Friedman proposes:

1. A hypothesis; (an explanation based on evidence) must be descriptively false

2. A hypothesis should take account of and account for no circumstances. (Circumstances are facts that are relevant to an event)

Friedman was attempting to defend economic models which are founded upon assumptions that do not match observations in the real world. He claims the models are successful. Therefore, the assumptions do not matter. Unfortunately, success is hard to come by since economic theories do not predict anything. A new price and quantity will occur, but economists cannot predict what they will be. They say the supply and demand curves move, establishing a new equilibrium point.

In the realm of science, a theory that does not predict anything is of little value. Karl Popper proposes that all

---

70 Milton Friedman, *Essays in Positive Economics*, Phoenix Books, 1966, page 14

scientific theories must be presented in a manner in which they can be proven false. Falsifiability avoids rationalization. Either the experimental results support the theory or they refute the theory.

"A theory which is not refutable by any conceivable event is nonscientific. Irrefutability is not virtue of a theory (as people often think) but a vice." [71]

In the mid-1900s, John Von Neumann, an extremely gifted mathematician, examined economic theory and proposed that the field needed to reconsider its dependence upon supply and demand curves. His suggestions were rebuffed:

"...an incident from the early 1940s in which von Neumann insisted at a seminar at Harvard that progress in economics would require a mathematics different from that which derived from the time of Newton. Samuelson challenged him then and remains defiantly unrepentant now:" [72]

The first thing a scientist needs to be is curious. They must be willing to test existing theories instead of defending them with rationalizations. They must be willing to find new ways to expand knowledge. The history of economics clearly shows that the economics profession does not operate in the same manner as a scientific community.

---

71   Karl R. Popper, *Conjectures and Refutations: The Growth of Scientific Knowledge*, Basic Books, New York, London 1962 page 37

72   Philip Mirowski, *Machine Dreams*, Cambridge University Press, 2002 Page 95

Symptom #4 Stereotyping Out Groups

The economists' favorite out group is the accounting profession. As discussed in Chapter 6, economists make the false claim that accountants do not track implicit costs. From Mankiw's book related to the discussion of opportunity costs:

> "By contrast, accountants have the job of keeping track of the money that flows into and out of firms. As a result, accountants measure the explicit costs but usually ignore the implicit costs."[73]

This is not true, and is perhaps why accountants generally disregard the economists, and vice versa. Recall from Chapter 6 that depreciation is an implicit cost that must be addressed for every accounting period. This is not something that can usually be ignored, as suggested by Mankiw.

Paul Samuelson's textbook begins with an excellent description of the income statement and balance sheet, fortunately a significant improvement over Mankiw's textbook. However, Samuelson introduces financial finagling, a situation where the accounting profession lacks judgement in treating certain items:

> ". . . we see that there is considerable judgement involved in determining the exact treatment of certain items. In the late 1990s, under pressure to produce rapidly growing earnings, many companies manipulated their accounts to show glowing results or to paper over losses."[74]

---

73 Gregory Mankiw, *Principles of Economics*, South-wester Cengage Learning, sixth edition page 261

74 Samuelson Nordhaus, *Economics*, McGraw Hill 18th edition, page 136

This is a significant disparagement of the accounting profession, and is a weak explanation of why the manipulation occurred. It wasn't pressure to produce growing earnings. It wasn't accountants acting on their own. Financial finagling was the result of an executive management team telling the accountants what to do in order to increase the executive bonus. The following comes from a competing economics book:

> "... A similar example of incentives for cheating comes from corporate finance. In the 1980s, chief executive officers (CEOs) were given much stronger incentives to increase their firm's stock price. Instead of being paid straight salary, they were awarded stock options. ... Enron and other scandals of the 1990s and the 2000s were, in part, the result." [75]

Samuelson goes on to explains how an economist's vision of business is superior to an accountant's view. This opinion is supported using the income statement from Hot Dog Ventures:[76] (See figure 1)

> "Hence, although the accountant might conclude that Hot Dog Ventures, with $37,000 in profits, is economically viable, the economist would pronounce that the firm is an unprofitable loser." [77]

Samuelson reaches the conclusion by considering that the owner is working sixty hours a week and is drawing no pay. To

---

75 Tyler Cowen, Alex Tabarrok, *Modern Principles of Economics*, Worth Publishers 2013 page 402

76 Samuelson Nordhaus ... page 134

77 Ibid, page 138

Income Statement Hot Dog Ventures INC		
Net Sales		$ 250,000
Costs of Goods Sold		
Materials	$ 50,000	
Labor Costs	$ 90,000	
Misc	$ 10,000	
Overhead		
Selling and Administrative	$ 15,000	
Rent	$ 5,000	
Depreciation	$ 15,000	
Total Operating		$ 185,000
Net Income		$ 65,000
Less		
Interest		$ 6,000
State and local Taxes		$ 4,000
Income before Income Taxes		$ 55,000
Corporate Income Tax		$ 18,000
Net Income after taxes		$ 37,000

Ch 8 Figure 1 – Hot Dog Ventures

think the accountant isn't aware that the owner is drawing no pay is not reflective of reality.

Samuelson wraps up his analysis with the following:

"A careful examination might show that Hot Dog Venture's owner could find a similar and equally interesting job working for someone else earning $60,000 a year."

It is most likely that the owner is very much aware of his choices, without the help of either an economist or an accountant.

Selecting accountants as the out group serves the purpose of distancing the economic theories away from the one group of people that would question the economists' odd mathematical conventions. It has been suggested that economists do not want young economists socializing or thinking with accountants, for fear their theories will be found lacking in realistic content.

Symptom #5 Pressure to Conform

One mechanism to exert pressure on economists is through the screening of papers that are published in the economic journals. Many economists who write papers that are not in line with the concept of supply and demand curves are excluded from such opportunities. Hiring of economists has also restricted thought, as economists who do not revere the classical theories find it more difficult to find employment. There is little interest in alternative thought.

An example includes Andre Gunder Frank, who lost his job at the University of Chicago early in his career due to his belief in and support of Keynesian economics:

> "Despite passing his comprehensive exams in economic theory and public finance after less than a year, Frank received a letter advising him to leave, because of his unsuitability." [78]

Psychological insight into this behavior is provided by two sources . . .

---

[78] David Seddon, *Andre Gunder Frank*, Obituary, The Independent http://www.independent.co.uk/news/obituaries/andre-gunder-frank-490030.html

Philip Tetlock, from the University of Pennsylvania, writes in his paper, *Sacred Values and Taboo Cognitions*:[79]

". . . humans prefer to believe that they have sacred values that provide firm foundations for their moral-political opinions. People can become very punitive "intuitive prosecutors" when they feel sacred values have been seriously violated, going well beyond the range of socially acceptable forms of punishment when given chances to do so covertly. . . ."

From Daniel B. Klein and Charlotta Stern—*Groupthink in Academia*

"Professors are likely to respect scholars who pursue questions similar to their own and who master similar modes of thought. They are not likely to respect scholars who pursue questions predicated on beliefs at odds with their own. Indeed, if a scholar is engaged in a task that might threaten a colleague's sense of self, he may give rise to personal distress and create acrimony between them."

"In academia, the beliefs are deep seated and connected to selfhood and identity. For that reason, protecting and preserving them have high personal stakes"[80]

The pressure to conform is significant.

---

79 Philip Tetlock, Thinking the unthinkable: sacred values and taboo cognitions, Trends in Cognitive Science, Vol7 no 7 July 2003

80 Daniel B Klein, Charlotta Stern, *Group Think in Academia, Majoritarian Department Politics and the Professional Pyramid*, The Independent Review V 13, Spring 2009

Symptoms #6 and #7—Self-Censorship and Mindguards

The economics department at a major university is an environment that mutes new ideas. From Klein/Stern;

> "The pyramid functions much like a genteel society in which criticism is muted. Particularly because of norms of consensus, it is impolitic to alienate colleagues. Going along to get along, dissidents and miscreants tend to suppress their disagreements with the dominant view, leading to what Timur Kuran calls "preference falsification".[81]

Steven Keen is an established scholar of economics, who believes the existing theories need to be replaced. He has written papers that are critical of Neoclassical Economics and provided the following comment from his book, *Debunking Economics*:

> "I have been unable to get the article published in neoclassical economics journals. The odds that this critique will ever be recognized by economics textbook writers are therefore effectively zero."[82]

Perhaps the most in-depth discussion of how academia enforced groupthink comes from Frederic Lee, a noted economist with over thirty years teaching experience:

---

81   Ibid

82   Steen Keen, *Debunking Economics*, Zed Books, 2011, page 100

"Dominance of Neoclassical Economics[83]

By 1970, there were over 15,000 American economists, most of whom were neoclassical economists and belonged to the AEA. Because of the repressive dominance of neoclassical economists, and because of the pre- and post-war repression of heterodox economics and economists, neoclassical economists shared membership in a tightly knit hierarchically-arrange community. This community accepted a single relatively homogeneous body of ideas or theories, shared the same set of standards—theoretical, technical and empirical—for evaluating research and hierarchically ranking publications, engaged in a network of inter-institutional and interpersonal ties that promoted communication, reciprocated employment and conference participation opportunities, and rejected or suppressed all else."

Lorrie Tarshis 1947

Perhaps the most striking example of mindguards comes from outside the economics profession. Lorrie Tarshis was a professor at Stanford University who had written one of the first successful textbooks for the education market, *The Elements of Economics*. Unfortunately, his text book was too favorable towards labor and the policies of the New Deal. This resulted in a political attack from a conservative group, "National Economic Council", led by Edwin Hart. The attack consisted of pamphlets written by Rose Wilder Lane, (co-founder of Libertarianism)

---

83 Frederic Lee, *A history of Heterodox Economics, Challenging the Mainstream in the Twentieth Century*, Routlege, 2009

to all University Trustees in the United States. Lane's pamphlet included . . .

"*The Elements of Economics* plays upon fear, shame, pity, greed, idealism, and hope to urge young Americans to act upon this theory as citizens. This is not an economics text at all; it is a pagan-religious and political tract." [84]

The result was a de-listing of Tarshis' book from the prescribed reading list. Needless to say, sales floundered and Tarshis reputation was harmed. [85]

It is worth comparing Samuelson and Tarshis in how they discussed labor unions in their respective economic books. Titles of the chapters are enough to tell the difference. Tarshis' chapter is "Labor". Samuelson's chapter title is "Labor Organizations and Problems".

Samuelson spends much of the chapter describing the ills associated with unions. He provides a scenario where a union member by the name of John Kennedy "has heard more than rumors to the effect that liquor gangsters "muscle in" on the union. . . ." [86] Samuelson continues with the description of a lawyer working for the union, and how busy he will be, given recent labor legislation. ". . . the lawyer is sure of only one thing,

---

84   Catherine Lawson, The "Textbook Controversy": Lessons for Contemporary Economics, AAUP Journal of Academic Freedom, Volume 6 2015

85   G C Harcourt, Obituary: *Professor Lorie Tarshis* 10/8/1993 (http://www.independent.co.uk/news/people/obituary-professor-lorie-tarshis-1509652.html

86   Paul Samuelson, *Economics*, first edition page 190, McGraw Hill, 1948

he and other lawyers on both sides are going to be kept awfully busy."[87]

Tarshis's language on labor included a more positive view of labor unions. "What unions do is to permit labor to meet monopoly with monopoly. Bargaining between a large corporation and the individual, unorganized worker, cannot be called competitive."[88]

The issue wasn't that Tarshis's book was too favorable towards communism, but that it was too favorable towards labor. Rose Wilder Lane and Edwin Hart were the thought police, effectively stamping out reasonable voices regarding labor unions in the time of McCarthyism.

Stanley Wong 1973

On occasion, the mindguards will miss the true topic of a paper and publish something they wish they had not. In 1973, Stanly Wong published a paper in *The American Economic Review* titled *"The "F-twist" and the Methodology of Paul Samuelson."* The article was a comparison of the two methodologies used by Milton Friedman and Paul Samuelson. Samuelson's methodology is referred to as descriptivism and Friedman's carries the name of instrumentalism. On the surface, the article seems like a friendly internal debate on how to frame the science of economics. However, the "F-Twist" article is actually a rejection of the methodologies used by all economists, as they fail to explain economic processes. Without an informative explanation, there is no theory.

---

87   Ibid page 193

88   Lorie Tarshis, *The Elements of Economics*, Houghton Mifflin Co, 1947, page 655

Recall, from Chapter 1, Francis Bacon's original work from 1620 and what is now known as the scientific method. Scientific methodology has four simple steps.

1. Observation and description of a phenomenon.

2. Formulation of a hypothesis to explain the phenomenon.

3. Use of the hypothesis to predict the existence of another phenomenon or predict quantitatively the results of new observations.

4. Independent experimentation to test and confirm the predictions, to support or refute the theory.

Economists do not follow these steps. There may be a law of supply that says suppliers will provide more if the price goes up, but no one has ever bothered to perform tests and experiments to validate the theory. They also have no quantitative elements in the law of supply. There is nothing to validate. The law cannot be proven or disproven.

Stanley Wong described Friedman's instrumentalism "methodology" with three steps:

A. A minimal set of assumptions that give rise to theory.

B. Theory is a set of axioms, postulates, or hypotheses that stipulate something about observable reality.

C. A set of consequences.

Scientists from other fields of study would reject the idea that assumptions are part of any scientific process. This was the source of Samuelson's argument with Friedman.

Similarly, Stanley Wong identified six steps for Samuelson's methodology of descriptivism:

1. Theory is just a description of observable experience.
2. Knowledge consists essentially of observational reports.
3. Explanations are ultimate.
4. Apriorism must be avoided.
5. Explanations turn out to be better descriptions.
6. All well-known theories in science are observations.

Samuelson is sorely missing the point. Theories explain things. They give reasons for why the pressure in the boiler goes up when heat is applied. Samuelson completely ignores cause and effect. He is satisfied with observations without understanding.

Economic descriptivism has no steps, no quantifiable values, no experimentation or testing. Using these six elements, if someone were to study the solar system, the result would be the Ptolemaic model, where everything revolved around the earth. The descriptive model actually did a relatively decent job of describing what was observed. Descriptive science shows "what," but it does not answer the question "why." Wong's words on descriptivism:

"According to *descriptivism,* of which Samuelson's methodology is a variant, a theory is just a description of observable experience, a convenient and mnemonic representation of empirical reality. Knowledge consists essentially of observational reports." [89]

---

89   Stanley Wong, "Foundations of Paul Samuelson's Revealed Preference Theory", Routledge, 2006, page 78

At the end of Stanley's F-Twist article, he asks for a methodology in economics that answers the question "why."

"The choice, then, is not between instrumentalism and descriptivism, but between them both and the view that a theory is explanatory and informative, one which provides an answer, albeit a tentative one, to the question, Why?"[90]

The role of mindguards for Stanley Wong is documented in his book *The Foundations of Paul Samuelson's Revealed Preference Theory*. The preface discusses obstacles that were erected to suppress his thoughts promoted by the "F-Twist" article. The first obstacle deals with Wong's doctoral thesis. The process was long and not without controversy. His PhD was finally awarded over a year after Stanley had submitted his dissertation.

Further evidence of suppression was encountered when Stanley attempted to publish other articles:

"Controversy did not end with the awarding of the PhD. While my dissertation was being considered by the examiners, I converted several chapters into articles and submitted them to various leading journals for consideration. All of them found the papers unacceptable."[91]

Stanley continued to face opposition in publishing his book *The Foundations of Paul Samuelson's Revealed Preference Theory.*

---

90   Stanley Wong, "The F-Twist and the methodology of Paul Samuelson", The American Economic Review, publisher American Economic Association, June 1973 PP 312-325

91   Stanley Wong, "Foundations of Paul Samuelson's . . . . "Page xvii

It took him several attempts to find a publisher. When it was finally published, American economic journals completely ignored the book:

"The book was very well received by reviewers for *Canadian Journal of Economics* (Winch, 1979), *Economica* (Jones-Lee, 1979), *Economic Journal* (Blaug, 1979), *Kyklos* (Hands, 1980) and *Manchester School* (Steedman, 1979). Oddly, the book was never reviewed in the *Journal of Economic Literature*, *Journal of Political Economy*, or any other American journal."[92]

It is not surprising the level of resistance, when considering an observation by a supporting economist:

". . . he had the chutzpah to confront one of the icons of the postwar neoclassical establishment and insist that the emperor had no clothes; and what's more, he did it calmly, with gravitas and style." [93]

Stanley Wong left the economics field in 1984:

"I left academic life because I felt the practice of law would enable me to satisfy my desire to have a practical challenge." [94]

---

92   Ibid page xviii

93   Ibid page xi

94   Ibid xxi

Leaders of Economic Thought Reject New Ideas

When Marshall's personality is factored in, it is easy to see how opposition to neoclassical thought would be suppressed at an early stage. J. M. Keynes provided this insight regarding Marshall's inability to entertain new ideas:

> "But his nervous equilibrium was easily upset by controversy and difference of opinion." [95]

> "Marshall was too much afraid of being wrong, too thin-skinned towards criticism, too easily upset by controversy even on matters of minor importance" [96]

Marshall's disposition was not supportive of new ideas. The best example is his refusal to meet H. L. Moore after Moore criticized Marshall in his paper *Economic Cycles, their Law and Cause*. His refusal to meet with Moore set neoclassical economics on the insular course that it still follows to this day.

The same concerns can be found in Paul Samuelson's inability to be skeptical about his own ideas. He was extremely intolerant of criticism and was more interested in arguing to support his position than in promoting knowledge. In his own words:

> "I lost my tolerance for global intransitivity, which came to smack of uninteresting formalism for its own sake. See Stanley Wong (1978) for related discussions. A reader of Philip Mirowski (1989) may find some difficulty in

---

95   J. M. Keynes, *Alfred Marshall* 1824-1924, page 326

96   Ibid page 345

reconciling remarks there and remarks here. Remark: The deep points raised by Dr. Wong can, I believe be argued out . . ."[97]

Samuelson's ego prevented him from considering other points of view. His entire focus was to argue against them.

Further evidence of how the group censors members today comes from Rod Hill and Tony Myatt, authors of *The Economics Anti-textbook*. The story is about a teaching assistant who is moved to another job due to her willingness to be critical about economic theory:

"However, at the end of December, I received an email from the administrator who was in charge of the TA assignments: I was being moved to another department entirely! It was felt that my 'radical teaching methods' were not a good fit for the economics department and would be 'better suited' to another discipline.

The professor quickly said this was not something to be debated in the course and moved on. I can only assume, then, that my unorthodox teaching became apparent through my students' willingness to think critically about the material." With "The professor quickly said this was not something to be debated in the course and moved on. I can only assume, then, that my unorthodox teaching became apparent through my students' willingness to think critically about the material." [98]

---

97   Stanley Wong, "Foundations of Paul Samuelson's xix

98   Rod Hill, Tom Myatt, Dealing with Dissent in the Classroom, June 21 2016, http://www.economics-antitextbook.com/

Freudian Concern?

The following excerpt comes from a book that recently won the Nobel Prize in Economics. The book is titled Nudge, written by Richard Thaler.

> "The great economist George Stigler once wrote an amusingly evil essay about an imaginary world in which students had the right to sue professors who taught them something that turned out to be wrong. The essay was called "A Sketch of the History of Truth in Teaching." [99] Professors shudder at the thought, but just imagine how much more expensive education would be today if universities and their employees had to carry mal-teaching insurance!"[100]

Perhaps the most stunning aspect of Stigler's article is that it was ever published. It is hard to imagine any scientific journal discussing truth in education in a humorous, sarcastic manner. Most people would assume truth to be an inherent part of any curriculum and would not be amused to discover professors wasting their time writing evil essays about truth in education.

However, Stigler's introductory lines show he is simply writing an article that opposes law suits that collect damages for defective products:

> "It started simply enough: various people—and especially a man named Nader—found automobiles less safe than

---

99 George Stigler, A Sketch of the History of Truth in Teaching, Journal of Political Economy, Vol 81, No 2, Mar-Apr 1973 pp 491-495

100 Richard H. Thaler and Cass R Sunstein, *Nudge Improving Decisions About Health, Wealth and Happines*, Penguin Books, 2009

they wished. . . . These zealous patrons of the public furthermore insisted that defective products be corrected."

At the end of Stigler's article, he jokes about the formation of a Federal Bureau of Academic Reading, Writing, and Research. The bureau would establish licensing to enforce honesty in Academia. Professors without a license could not obtain insurance against suits for incompetence and would be driven from teaching. Oddly enough, in Stigler's imaginary world, professors in economic development were unable to obtain such license.

Conclusion:

The economics profession during the 1900s was a closed, tight knit group that actively managed thought and opinion within its ranks. Groupthink was firmly in place, preventing the development of true knowledge in preference for an ideology that cannot be questioned.

This attitude would be counter to any scientific community that promotes:

Skepticism: Great effort is expended to test and validate current information and replace it with better information.

Refutability/Falsifiability—All theories must be subject to experimentation for either support or rejection.

Pluralism—No central arbiter of truth. Theories and proofs stand on their own merit. All parties can equally contribute to the knowledge base.

None of these three attributes can be ascribed to economists.

CHAPTER 9

Better Lessons Learned

"The goal of education is the advancement of knowledge and the dissemination of truth."

—John F. Kennedy.

MOST OF THIS book has been focused on identifying the lack of truth in economic theory. Syllogisms and mathematical card tricks hide the ideological foundation for supply and demand curves. Students, our children, are confused by the tricks and believe that economics is truly a scientific presentation of knowledge.

Capitalism, with appropriate balancing forces, is a successful sociological structure for advancing human prosperity, and should no longer be threatened by competing ideologies such as communism or socialism. However, we need to be honest with our children and society about how capitalism works, and what balancing forces are required.

Our largest social failure experienced by teaching supply and demand curves is that our children are not taught how to prosper in the economic dimension of life. Students do not learn about credit, debt, career management, net worth, risk management, or other critical knowledge and skills they need. These topics are covered in a class called Financial Literacy. Unfortunately, most parents are clueless about what is taught in an economics class. They assume an economics class addresses financial literacy; but, it does not and it cannot. Instead, our children take an economics class that teaches one what to think, not how to think. In some states, students are forced to take the class, as it is a high school graduation requirement. An economics class can be compared to teaching someone what a fish is instead of teaching them how to catch a fish. The sad part is teaching someone what a fish is does not even feed them for a day.

The only logical conclusion is to change the high school curriculum by dropping economics in favor of financial literacy.

Relevance

The quality or state of being closely connected or appropriate, the perception that something is interesting and worth knowing.

Students despise classes that seem to be irrelevant to their life pursuits. Psychologists know that relevance can make or break a student's ability to learn a given topic. Without relevance, there is no self-motivation.

Parents want their children to be successful in life. They want the curriculum to be relevant and useful. They depend upon their state legislature and state school boards to set a curriculum that prepares their children for life in today's world.

Teachers want to educate their students. They understand that knowledge and truth must go hand in hand. They are unaware of the false science promoted by economics.

The relevant material that allows our children to prosper is the material contained in a financial literacy class.

Financial Literacy

Many states and organizations have worked to define the course content for financial literacy. A short yet fairly complete list would include.

1. Budgeting and planning for financial needs.
2. Saving and investing to support financial goals
3. Credit, debt and credit scores
4. Reading markets, shopping, and negotiating
5. Careers and Income
6. Risk, Insurance and legal matters
7. Housing and home ownership as an investment
8. Taxation, public spending, social security and retirement.

In addition to these topics there should be outside reading assignments of books about real life economics. Possible books could include; The Crash of 1929, The Smartest Men in the Room, Boomerang, When Genius Failed, Random Walk Down Wall Street, Inside Job, Charles Schwab's Guide to Investing, Think and Grow Rich, Seven Habits of Highly Effective People and The Total Money Makeover.

A typical course would use a book with about 14 chapters and would last about one semester or eighteen weeks. Additional knowledge and skills that would as a pre-requisite would include use of Excel for building spreadsheets for budgeting and financial modeling.

This material is extremely relevant and useful; however, only four states, (UT, TN, VA, and MO) require the course for high school graduation. If a parent, teacher, or student, were given the choice between learning financial literacy or economics, most would choose financial literacy.

Why hasn't the curriculum changed?

The Establishment

The people that run this country, at the national level and the state level, like things just the way they are. They prefer consumers and labor to be misinformed, timid, and malleable. To support this conclusion, all one needs to do is examine what happens at the state level, with the legislative bodies that control the educational system. There are five tactics employed by politicians to keep education away from our children.

Tactic #1—Let it Die

Florida was recently credited with promoting a bill that would require financial literacy as a graduation requirement. Even though the bill had unanimous approval from all of the reviewing committees, it died.

> **Last Action:** 5/5/2017 House—Indefinitely postponed and withdrawn from consideration—Died on Calendar[101]

Tactic #2—All for Show

Another tactic employed is to pass a bill that requires the class to be part of the curriculum, but not a requirement for graduation. Ed Hernandez in California trumpeted success that never occurred:[102]

> "With this new law, California requires financial literacy to be taught as part of the official state curriculum . . ."

---

101 https://www.flsenate.gov/Session/Bill/2017/00955

102 Adolfo Guzman Lopez. Despite New Law, California lags in personal finance. 5/6/2016. http://www.scpr.org/news/2016/05/06/60317/despite-new-law-california-lags-in-personal-financ/

"But the law did not actually require any basic money management skills to be taught, and three years later, personal finance instruction in California remains a patchwork effort often totally reliant on the efforts of individual schools or teachers."

Tactic # 3—Bury the Class

A third tactic is to require financial literacy to be taught, but allow it to be part of another course. Data from the Council for Economic Education[103] reported that seventeen states required personal finance. (See figure 1) However, thirteen of the seventeen allowed financial literacy to be part of another course. As mentioned, time to effectively teach the subject needs to be allowed, as the time required to teach financial literacy requires a full semester and a specifically trained instructor. A closer look at Arizona's solution reveals extremely weak specification for content of such a course. The following comes from the school district serving Prescott, AZ.[104]

"This class will be an introduction to micro and macroeconomics. Students will study economic concepts such as supply and demand, monetary and fiscal policy, inflation, personal finance, as well as an in-depth look at the American Stock Exchange. Students will be required to complete a mock stock portfolio project. Students will

---

103 Survey of the States, Economic and Personal Finance Education in or Nation's Schools 2016, Council for Economic Education

104 http://www.prescottschools.com/phs/wp-content/uploads/ sites/22/2017/01/course-descriptions-2017-18.pdf

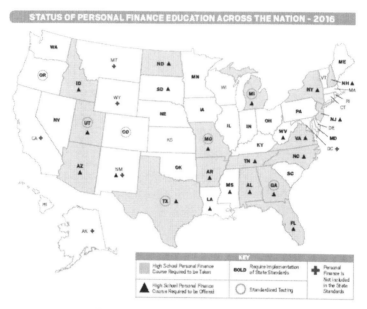

Ch 9 Figure 1 – Survey of the States

gain a practical understanding of our economic system as well as an introduction into other world systems. Students will also spend time exploring personal finance and its practical applications."

There is no way the Arizona content will address the needs for financial literacy. In the state of Utah, the person who teaches financial literacy does not teach economics.

Our children and parents are being sold a bill of goods when states allow personal finance to be merged with any other class. This method of burying the material in a class about ideology is a significant threat to obtaining true knowledge.

Tactic #4 Fail to Fund

Many states will pass laws requiring the course, but they do not provide funding to cover the cost of things like instructor training or books. As an example, in 2017, California was preparing a law proposing the course, and funding; but, the law was modified to strip funding. The following was removed from the original bill early in the legislative process:

> This bill would add a course in financial literacy to the list of courses a pupil is required to complete to receive a diploma of graduation from high school on and after January 1, 2019. Because the bill would impose additional duties on local educational agencies, the bill would impose a state-mandated local program.
>
> The California Constitution requires the state to reimburse local agencies and school districts for certain costs mandated by the state. Statutory provisions establish procedures for making that reimbursement.
>
> This bill would provide that, if the Commission on State Mandates determines that the bill contains costs mandated by the state, reimbursement for those costs shall be made pursuant to the statutory provisions noted above.[105]

The bill was further watered down by removing the graduation requirement making the course an elective that could replace economics as a requirement for graduation. The bill died and was never voted on by either house. Both democrats and republicans were involved in proposing and neutering the bill.

---

105 https://leginfo.legislature.ca.gov/faces/billNavClient.xhtml?bill_id=201720180SB583

Tactic #5 Confuse the Public

In the example above from California, at one point the revised bill was modified so that it does not require anything for graduation that is not part of admission requirements for the University of California. Checking the University admission requirements shows that financial literacy is not required. The bill confuses the public.

It is no accident that financial literacy is not taught in our high schools. For all fifty states, only four have actively promoted a curriculum that teaches our children how to prosper in a capitalist society. If parents don't complain, nothing will change.

Why your University is not on your side

In addition to political forces at the state level resisting change, there is resistance in the academic arena. Universities are homes of the groupthink society that created the false science of economics. They are active proponents of the ideology and extend their influence to the high school arena through the AP College Board testing services. Students can be financially rewarded by taking an AP Economics Class. If a student can pass an AP exam, they can eliminate a required college course for graduation. The cost/value of an economics class is about $2,000 at a public university. The AP College Board charges about $100 for the test. With over 200,000 students taking Micro and Macro Economics tests each year, the annual revenue for the College Board is over $20 million. The students' avoided cost at the university level is over $400 million annually.

Consider Long Beach Polytechnic High School, which at one time offered a semester-long course on personal finance:

The class was cancelled this year after an enrollment drop.

"There's a big push throughout the country to do AP tests," Adler said. "Kids have to ask, can I take this regular class or do I need to take another AP?' The majority of kids have to choose the APs if they're trying to get into really good colleges."[106]

There is no AP test for financial literacy. Therefore, top students will take a different course in order to improve their chances of getting accepted at the best college possible. Parents are unaware that economics classes are of little value.

It is difficult to even imagine the amount of money universities collect teaching supply and demand curves. If you assume that AP exams accounted for only 20% of the population that would be required to take an economics class, the number of students taking basic economics would be about 800,000 a year. If the cost per class for a student is $2,000, the total annual revenue reaches a whopping $1.6 billion a year.

In addition to financial motivation at Universities and the AP College board, there is a large population of teachers and professors teaching economics. The resistance to change becomes obvious. These people have no incentive to impartially compare the value of a financial literacy course with the value of an economics class. The academic system is biased for the status quo.

Corporate Influence in Academia

Universities today collect billions of dollars in donations from corporations that promote conservative ideals. The poster child

---

106 Ibid Adolfo Guzman-Lopez

for their ideology is Neoclassical Economics, featuring supply and demand curves. Lawrence C. Soley's book, *Leasing the Ivory Tower*, provides a wealth of information on how corporations use academia to promote their goals and ideology.

> "... Universities are obliged by their corporate funders to fill endowed professorships with individuals whom corporate contributors find acceptable. These are usually corporate cheerleaders, political conservatives, or deregulation advocates such as Sam Peltzman, the Sears Roebuck Professor of Economics at the University of Chicago, Peltzman is a vociferous opponent of business regulation and a former staff economist with President Nixon ..." [107]

Often, economics professors operate outside the sphere of their parent universities, yet they use the university as an informal legitimization of the positions they promote. An example from the University of Texas would include Lewis Spellman, who publishes the *Spellman Report*.

> "*The Blog* is a reflection of Professor Spellman's views and teaching that has taken place at the University of Texas in Finance, Law, and the LBJ School of Public Affairs. He has also taught at Stanford University and UC-Berkeley".

---

107 Lawrence C. Soley, *Leasing the Ivory Tower*, South End Press, 1995
    page 128

Spellman uses his position of authority at the University to spread false stories about progressive politicians, most notably Lyndon Johnson. Consider the following excerpt from an article written by Spellman:

> "1965 was a momentous year for the US. LBJ, the newly elected President, was in a bind. He had objectives that required spending, which would generate a fiscal deficit—and, in turn, more government debt. . . .
>
> (To avoid the debt . . .)
>
> . . . A way was found, and it's still used today. The Federal Government would raid any pot of taxpayer money set aside for another purpose and spend it—and then cover it up. . . .
>
> This is the general mechanics of what has occurred on a grand scale with the social insurance trust funds. The particular pot of money most tempting for the government to raid for other use was the Social Security "trust" fund. That's because it was large and growing, at the time, as the Baby Boomers were just entering the labor force hence contributing to the Social Security trust funds via the payroll tax.
>
> What made Social Security funds even more a target was that the great majority of the beneficiaries wouldn't be scheduled to receive promised benefits for decades. That is, the missing funds would not be missed for some time."[108]

---

108 Lewsi Spellman, The Spellman Report, For the Millennials, The Social Security Chickens Have Come Home to Roost,

Spellman alleges that LBJ raided the social security trust fund in order to pay for the Vietnam War and social programs without running a deficit. This is not true. The social security trust fund has never been raided[109]. Spellman fails to include the fact that the introduction of Medicare and Medicaid in 1965 was funded with new taxes. He also confuses people about the trust fund, and makes people think the money is gone, when in reality it has been invested in government bonds. Nobody in their right mind would save $2.6 trillion dollars and put it under the mattress. They would use the money to buy an investment and the safest investment in the USA is federal government debt.

All economists should understand that placing your cash savings under a mattress is a poor decision. Considering the rate of inflation, and the advantages of compounding, had the cash collected by the social security system been kept under a mattress, it would probably only total $600 billion. That would be a loss of $1.8 trillion. People who claim the trust fund has been raided are trying to confuse the public and demonize the federal government.

It seems ironic that a professor teaching at the LBJ School of Public Affairs could make such a statement about LBJ without any repercussions from his employer. Spellman should at least be required to provide evidence of Johnson's larceny. Academia allows the charade to continue by distancing themselves from personal blogs while at the same time collecting donations from corporations that are effectively paying for the desired press.

Any university that supports such activities is not operating in the public's best interest. If Universities do not protect and promote the truth, who will? Perhaps any think tank associated

109 https://www.ssa.gov/history/InternetMyths2.html

with a university should be shut down or be required to sever all ties, including cross employment, with the parent university.

Call for Change

Two things must be done to help society improve its understanding about how to prosper in a capitalistic system.

1. All states need to require financial literacy as a course for high school graduation.

2. Economics, founded upon supply and demand curves, needs to be either dropped from the educational environment or should be accompanied with a warning label similar to "The concept of supply and demand curves does not meet the standards for scientific study."

Consider the three most affected parties:

1. Students

2. Parents

3. Unsuspecting Teachers

Students

High school students should work together to demand change. Challenge your local school board by asking for time to raise the concern at a school board meeting. Tell them you need to learn financial literacy in order to be successful. Let your parents know your plans as well. Start a club at your high school called Financial Literacy for Prosperity. Students have the right to demand relevant education. If all else fails, file a request to remove economics from your personal graduation requirements due to religious beliefs. Pursuit of self-interest and profits above all else is counter to many basic religious teachings.

Be an entrepreneur—do what is right for you.

College level students must do the same, with even louder voices. Organize a group to promote financial literacy. Petition your university or college to offer a class in Financial Literacy as a replacement for any course in Economics. Organize for change as one student alone will not have an effect, while a petition signed by thousands cannot be ignored.

Parents

Parents will play a key role in changing the high school environment. Parents are best positioned to apply pressure on local school officials and state legislators. Parents need to be clear about their demand—"teach our children how to prosper in our capitalistic system". Prosperity only comes from understanding relevant fundamental economic practices, as covered in a financial literacy course. Attend your local school board meeting and request change. Write your principal with the same request. Do not be satisfied with any excuses. Just as the students can organize for change, so can adults. If the school claims they don't have books or trained staff, there are nonprofit organizations like Jumpstart that can help through purchasing books and providing volunteers to train teachers.

Apply pressure on your state representative. Organize meetings at your school and invite your representative to hear your concerns. Ask your political party for clear support for this change. Both parties should agree that learning financial literacy is more important than moving around imaginary supply and demand curves. Stand up for what you need.

Unsuspecting Teachers

For those teachers who never questioned the theories of economics, these ideas may come as a shock. The scientific charade was a well-hidden secret. Now is the time to obtain certification for a class that will truly make a difference in someone's life. Your students will learn the basics of managing their financial life. Take this challenge as a personal opportunity. Let your administration know that you are willing and able to take on the task. If your state lags in addressing the problem and still requires economics, ask the parents to choose between supply and demand vs personal finance and teach what the parents want. If the school refuses to help the students and parents, teach the course after hours.

Be an entrepreneur—provide what society needs. Negotiate a price and make it happen.

Role of Science Organizations

Scientific organizations must stand up and identify the faults in economic theory to strip away the veil of scientism. Staying silent is part of the problem. Support from organizations such as the American Science Affiliation, the Federation of American Scientists, and the National Coalition for Universities in the Public Interest is required for this movement to be successful. At the international level, the Max Planck Institute and the Nobel Prize organization should defend the definition of science and remove supply and demand based theories from any association with scientific process.

Any organization that uses science as a facade for ideology is a threat to all science.

CHAPTER 10

Improved Vision

"... financial statements should present information that is as useful as possible to investors, creditors and others in assessing the future prospects of a business—the basis for all economic decisions."[110]

—Norman O. Olson

STUDENTS WHO HAVE been trained in financial literacy have learned the true mathematical language of economics: accounting and finance. Just like physic uses trigonometry and calculus to observe and model physical phenomenon, economics uses accounting and finance to observe, model and manage economic activity. All business decisions are based upon two fundamental accounting reports, the balance sheet and the income statement. This information in conjunction with financial rules that provide guidance on how to account for time, provide the basis for economic decisions.

---

110 George R. Catlett and Norman O Olson, In Pursuit of Professional Goals, Arthur Anderson and Co. Chicago, 1973, page 172, Testimony of George Catlett and Norman O. Olson at public hearing.

Measurable Economics

Measurable economics focuses on two aspects:

1. Money/value in motion
2. Money/value at rest.

Money in motion is captured in a firm's income statement, or a family budget, while money/value at rest is recorded in a firm's balance sheet or reflected in a household's net worth. All financial literacy classes should provide the basic description of an income statement and a balance sheet.

An income statement may also be referred to as the P&L which stands for Profit and/or Loss statement or a statement of operations. There are three key elements in a basic income statement: (See figure 1)

1. Income = incoming dollars
2. Expenses = outgoing dollars
3. Net Income = Income – expenses

It is important to note some terms have different meanings in different situations. Income for an individual is salary and income for a business is revenue or sales. Net income and profit are terms used by a business and are equivalent to savings for an individual.

A balance sheet also has three distinct elements. (See figure 2)

1. Assets
2. Liabilities
3. Net worth or stockholder's equity

All economic entities have a balance sheet that reflects an estimated value of assets, liabilities and net worth at a specific

Household or Firm Budget	
Income/Revenue/Salary/Sales	$50,000
Expenses	-$40,000
Net income/Savings/Profit	$10,000

Ch 10 Figure 1 – Budgeting

Household Balance Sheet	
Things we own	$250,000
Obligations/debt	-$200,000
Networth/Stockholders equity	$50,000

Ch 10 Figure 2 – Balance Sheet

point in time. It is important to highlight that the value or price for any asset can only be estimated. This presents an inherent deficiency for economic reporting on the balance sheet. Just as two consumers may value the same car at different amounts, the price actually paid is unknown until a sale is made. The accounting profession works to minimize this deficiency by providing standard guidance on how to value assets.

The rest of this chapter assumes that firms and households are following realistic methods to estimate the values of items on a balance sheet. For example, a household would place a reasonable market value on their home and businesses would report reasonable market values for assets owned by the business.

Measuring a Firm's Ecosystem

The firm's ecosystem has five primary players. The firm, the employees, the providers of raw materials for the business, the providers for goods to the families, and the buyers of products from the firm. The benefit of this model is that everything

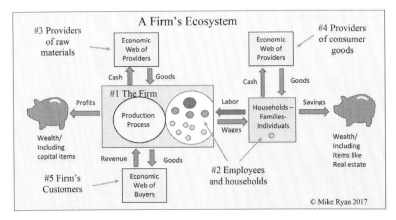

Ch 10 Figure 3 – Firm's Ecosystem

represented by an arrow is measurable. Notice that goods flow in one direction and money flows in the opposite direction. All of these items would be reflected on an income statement for the firm or a budget or ledger for a family. The contents of the piggy banks would be recorded on a balance sheet. (See figure 3)

All economic entities, such as the firm, the families, the buyers, and customers, are living in the economic dimension of society. In the economic dimension, bankruptcy is the equivalent to death. If a firm is not profitable, the firm will drain wealth reserves and eventually go out of business. If a household's expenses exceed its wages, it will also eventually go bankrupt. Survival in an economic sense is similar to survival in a biologic sense. Economic entities will pursue all sorts of survival strategies in order to stay alive.

Notice that employees have a symbiotic relationship with their employer. The employer is powerless without labor, and labor will starve without a healthy host. The firm depends upon a healthy labor pool to reach its production goals. In this simple representation, there are three classes of labor shown on the diagram. Production workers are represented by the small circles, while management is a larger circle, and the owners or executive team is shown as the largest circle.

The model reveals the paradoxical relationship between production workers and owners/executives. The firm must pay the labor pool enough to provide a prosperous family environment. If the firm can pay them less, the firm's profits will increase at the expense of family wealth accumulation for the worker. If management pays them too much, profits could erode or disappear, driving the firm out of business. The urge to increase profits is significant in the capitalistic system. Publicly traded firms are under constant pressure to grow profits. There is no easy answer or any equation or natural law that tells management the wage labor rate for workers. Management is left with the dilemma of balancing profits for the owners vs savings for the families. Given managers works for owners, the outcome is predictable. Perhaps a natural law of wages might be written as: If the owner is pursuing self-interest, the workers will be paid less.

Impact of Minimum Wage

Economists and employers want workers to believe that minimum wage is harmful to the workers. This concept is taught using supply and demand curves as the justification.[111] (See figure 4)

---

111 Gregory Mankiw, Economics, page 118

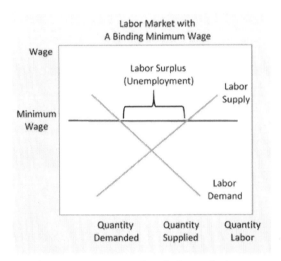

Ch 10 Figure 4 – Mankiw "Chartist" Theory

"Because the minimum wage is a price floor, it causes a surplus: The quantity of labor supplied exceeds the quantity demanded. The result is unemployment."

With a quick review of the ecosystem, an increase in wages by $1, results in an extra $1 in the family budget, which will either be spent on goods or added to savings. The other effect is that profits for the firm decrease by $1. The effect on the number of people employed does not exist if the firm is still profitable.

Consider an example using a pro forma income statement from a McDonalds' franchise.[112] The income statement shows a profit of $163,900. For this discussion, we will assume the labor crew is currently being paid at the rate of $11/hr. (See figure 5)

---

112 http://www.mymoneyblog.com/mcdonalds-franchise-cost-vs-
    profit.html

Income Statements for Three Conditions	
Net sales	2,700,000
Food Costs	-810,000
Rent and Frachise fees	-391,500
Crew Labor @ $11/hr	-540,000
Other Expenses	-794,600
Total Operating Income	163,900
Net sales	2,700,000
Food Costs	-810,000
Rent and Frachise fees	-391,500
Crew Labor @15/hr	-736,364
Other Expenses	-794,600
Total Operating Income	-32,464
Net sales + 7.4%	2,899,800
Food Costs	-810,000
Rent and Frachise fees	-391,500
Crew Labor @15/hr	-736,364
Other Expenses	-794,600
Total Operating Income	167,336

Ch 10 Figure 5 – Various Impacts on Profit

If a financial literacy student were asked to describe the impact of raising the minimum wage to $15, an increase of 36%, they would first report labor costs would rise to $736,364. (an increase of $190k) The student would also report that if the business holds "all things equal", the result would be a loss of $32,464.

The student would continue by proposing a possible response, such as raising the price of burgers by 7.4% in order to reestablish previous profit levels. This would result in the price of a big mac meal going from $6.00 to $6.44. Some may raise concerns about inflation for hamburger prices, but the worker is better off as his/her wage went up 36%.

A common concern is that customers will respond to the price increase by going elsewhere for their burgers, resulting in a sales drop. However, since all other franchises are facing the same increase in minimum wage, that should not be a major concern, as prices have also gone up at Burger King and other competitors. In the worst case, some of the customers may elect to cook their own burgers at home, and a small sales drop might be expected.

Another strategy for the owner would be to negotiate better deals with their providers and cut costs. Notice that Food Costs and Rent/Franchise fees all come from the McDonalds corporate office and total about $1.2 million. A reduction of this cost by about 16% would save the $190k and restore the profits of the franchise. This would be strongly opposed by McDonalds corporate, as a drop in sales of 16% would have a large inpact on their profits and stock price.

With improved vision, the dynamic market response to a wage increase is far more complicated than concluding the result is unemployment. More wages to the workers means less profits to the owners or higher prices in the market or cost cutting with suppliers or some combination of actions.

An alternative thought provoking question might be why has the cost of a burger almost doubled since the last minimum wage hike. If the workers have not received a pay raise since 2009, is it due to owners keeping an expanded flow of profits? Given the stock price has tripled, it does make one wonder.

Academic Response

Seattle recently passed laws to raise the minimum wage within the city from $11/hour to $13/hr and finally to $15/hr with the final raise happening in mid-2017. Two studies have been released, and each study reached different conclusions. A University of Washington study claimed the following:

"The effects of dis-employment appear to be roughly offsetting the gain in hourly wage rates, leaving the earnings for the average low-wage worker unchanged."[113]

If the earnings were unchanged, that implies that the worker take home pay is the same while working fewer hours. If someone were to ask the worker if things were changed, they would say: "This is great, I earn the same wages in 29 hours when it used to take the full 40-hour work week." A positive result for the worker. If in fact the restaurant were already operating at maximum efficiency, the total hours would not be reduced and the take home pay would rise.

However, the study did not survey the employers or the employees to reach any conclusion. Instead, the study tried to compare employment in Seattle to employment in other cities in Washington. The study went so far as to create a "Synthetic Seattle" to perform an analysis, including people earning as much as $19 an hour. The predicted dis-employment totaled 5,000 people. Notice this is a predicted impact, not a measured impact.

Why bother with a prediction when it is possible to measure the results by conducting a pay survey of those now earning the increased rate? Why didn't the study track employment hours and wages in Seattle before and after the change? Recall from Chapter 9, that academia is financially motivated to use supply

---

113 The Seattle Minimum Wage Team, Report on the impact of Seattle's Minimum Wage, July 2016 University of Washington

and demand curves, and that supply and demand curves predict unemployment. Any study that reaches a different conclusion would show the theories are incorrect. Don't be satisfied with the newspaper headlines. Track down the original report and read it with a critical eye.

Wages and Wealth

A closer look at the firm's ecosystem and associated money flows shows why businesses and conservative think tanks do not want to raise wages. Every dollar saved on paying the labor crew represents increased profit. (See figure 6)

This model also shows that profits for the firm and savings for the household are very comparable. Household savings and corporate profits are the two items that contribute to a growing wealth pool. No savings, no profits, no wealth build up. Be aware that economists get confused when discussing wages, often referring to them as the profit from labor. This is not a fair comparison. That would be like calling revenue "profits".

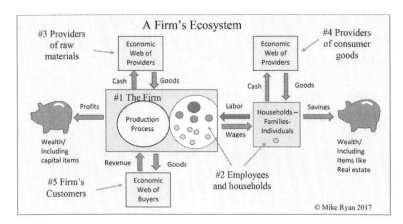

Ch 10 Figure 6 – Firm's Ecosystem

Consider the following comment from a writer from the Adam Smith Institute:

"Nurses get paid, don't they? That's a profit from their labour isn't it?"[114]

Nope. Profits are only found after subtracting costs. Even Adam Smith knew that laborers had costs to pay. In fact, Adam Smith predicted that workers would have no profits/savings as they would only be paid enough to cover food, clothing, and housing.

"The ordinary or average price of provisions determines the quantity of money which must be paid to the workman" [115]

The terminology is somewhat confusing. Recall that income for an individual is salary and income for a business is revenue or sales. Net income and profit are terms used by a business that are equivalent to savings for an individual. If an individual owns their own home, the mortgage could be viewed as a form of savings, as it contributes to wealth accumulation. If an individual is renting, their housing expense does not contribute to wealth accumulation. These concepts would be taught in a financial literacy course.

---

114 Tim Worstall, Milton Friedman Told us the Answer Decades Ago, Comments Forbes, June 4, 2017

115 Adam Smith, Wealth of Nations, Metalibri Digital edition, 2007 Page 671

In *Wealth of Nations*, Adam Smith recognized there are three different forms of wages.[116]

1. Labor Wages—money paid to workers to create product or service

2. Inspection and Direction Wages—Money paid to management team

3. Capital wages—money paid to the owner of the business, who provided the capital to launch and operate the business

In Adam Smith's day, with sole proprietors, the owner received the wages for Inspection and Direction as well as the capital wages. For the corporate shareholder, capital wages constitutes the return on their financial investment, which is different than capital investment. The fundamental difference between financial investing and capital investing is beyond the scope of this book. Future books from this series will spend time exploring the two types of investing.

This situation results in wealth creation being driven predominantly by profits. A $100 dividend generally goes into savings, while a $100 wage is predominantly spent on consumables. The relevant observation is one of the key features for any economic system.

#1: Ownership has the privilege of a larger portion of wealth creation.

That does not make ownership a bad thing. From Pope Leo in 1893:

---

116 Ibid page 42

"Private ownership, as we have seen, is the natural right of man, and to exercise that right, especially as members of society, is not only lawful, but absolutely necessary."[117]

Pope Leo also noted a responsibility carried by owners of capital:

"Justice, therefore, demands that the interests of the working classes should be carefully watched over by the administration, so that they who contribute so largely to the advantage of the community may themselves share in the benefits which they create-that being housed, clothed, and bodily fit, they may find their life less hard and more endurable "[118]

Pope Leo was a firm believer in minimum wage and some mechanism for society to watch over the rights of workers. The only mechanisms available today are government regulations or unions to represent the workers. Without such countervailing force, workers will find themselves discarded in favor of profits for the owners.

Unfortunately, the relationship between owner and employee today is not what Adam Smith experienced. Today, ownership is entirely isolated from the employee. There is little awareness of human condition. The owner of a share of McDonalds is detached from the personal plight of the workers across America. The stockholder only sees a financial asset that is performing its duty of generating profits, the more the better.

117 Pope Leo XIII, Rerum Novarum, 1891
118 Ibid

Thus, a second observation regarding the nature of all modern economic systems is uncovered:

#2: The anonymous relationship between owner and laborer in the corporate environment obscures the condition of the labor class from the ownership class.

From Pope Francis:

> "The principal ethical dilemma of this capitalism is the creation of discarded people, then trying to hide them, or make sure they are no longer seen," the Pope continued. "A serious form of poverty in a civilization is when it is no longer able to see its poor, who are first discarded and then hidden."[119]

Someone trying to live on a minimum wage of $7.25 has roughly $15,000 a year to spend, assuming 40-hour work weeks. This is near the poverty line, which qualifies the employee for government subsidies in the form of Earned Income Tax Credits, and probably other programs such as discounted healthcare. It makes more sense that the employee's firm should pay a livable wage and not require assistance from the government to feed and clothe its employees. The government assistance is effectively a subsidy to the various industries that fail to pay a livable wage.

> "The two biggest welfare queens in America today are Wal-Mart and McDonald's."[120]

---

119 Pope Paul VI, Economy of Communion, Vatican, 2/4/17

120 Barry Ritholtz, "How McDonalds and Walmart became Welfare Queens". Forbs 11/13/2013

A solution that restores human dignity is a higher minimum wage. Arguments against the minimum wage can be partially addressed by employing a tiered minimum wage based upon characteristics such as age, family status or location. A livable wage in New York City is significantly different from a livable wage in small town USA. A working parent paid less than a livable wage will not have the money or time to properly raise their family. A student living at home could make ends meet with a smaller livable wage.

Profits at All Costs

Another characteristic from the firm's ecosystem to consider is what different pressures are experienced by the different classes of worker. The ownership/executive class works under tremendous pressure to perform, much like the pressures faced by an Olympic athlete:

> "Long hours, crushing workloads, multiple and constant pressures, and incessant conflict and unpopularity often come with the job."[121]

To thrive, executives and owners must be competitive, hard-working, and relentless. They deserve tremendous credit for being able to guide a corporation the same way a skilled horseman rides a horse. They are surrounded by other executives with the same pressures. They are all paid to make tough decisions, such as moving production to China in order

---

121 Carl Bueke PhD," How do Executives Survive", Psychology Today, 2/27/12

to cut costs. This provides a third observation for the modern economic system:

#3: Corporate leadership is rewarded for growing profits at all costs.

As noted by Milton Friedman:

> "... there is one and only one social responsibility of business—to use its resources and engage in activities designed to increase its profits so long as it stays within the rules of the game, which is to say, engages in open and free competition without deception or fraud."[122]

The difficulty with the third observation are the two words all cost. When it comes to environmental costs, these are typically imposed upon other citizens who must live with the pollution or clean up the pollution. Corporations will avoid the cost of preventing pollution in order to grow profits. Corporations will avoid labor costs by moving production out of a country to grow profits. The costs imposed upon the community due to lost jobs is not a concern for the corporation.

Milton Friedman was correct, corporations avoid any and all costs that they can, including avoiding a fair tax in order to expand profits. Avoidance strategies are generally available to any lobbying organization in Washington that has the money required to influence legislation. Blind pursuit of self-interest has costs that cannot be paid for by the invisible hand.

---

122 Milton Friedman, *Capitalism and Freedom*, University of Chicago press, 1982 page 112

Unions as Taught in a US Economics Textbook

Economic text books want workers to believe that unions are bad for other workers, and provide no benefit for workers in a union. From Paul Samuelson's 18th edition:[123]

1. If unions succeed in raising their wages . . . their gains come at the expense of wages of nonunion workers. . . .

2. We can see no appreciable impact on unionization on the share of wages in the United States.

3. Above equilibrium wages, whether caused by minimum wage laws or unions . . . result(s) in a surplus of labor or unemployment.[124]

The ownership class wants people to believe false economic theory as it furthers their self-interest by leaving more profits in their pockets and less savings for the working class. Given there are no supply and demand curves, and no equilibrium wage, this theory can be discarded.

Conclusion

With improved vision, citizens can ask their own questions and reach their own conclusions.

If people and corporations pursue their own self-interest, with the single responsibility to increase profits, with no consideration for fellow man or the environment, the outcome will be lower

123 Paul Samuelson, *Economics*, 18th edition, McGraw Hill, 2005 page 256

124 Gregory Mankiw, *Principles of Economics*, 6th edition, South-Western Cengage Learning, 2012, page 405

wages, government deficits, a degrading environment and income inequality. Without society providing opposing forces to economic self-interest of powerful corporations, the living conditions for society will degrade. There are no market solutions that curb self-interest. Regulation is a fact of life for an equitable society, as regulations provide the balancing forces that curb the natural tendency for avarice found in all economic systems.

Epilog

"... What lies behind the veil of economics? Vision and ideology."

—Robert Heilboner

THE PRIMARY POINT of this book is to shine a bright light on our educational system and inform students, parents, teachers and citizens that there is a better choice for our children's curriculum. It will be very interesting to see how different people in society react to this suggestion. What groups will support the change and what groups will resist? Which states will move the quickest to correct a glaring problem? Common sense suggests one legislative session is all that is required. However, society is not ruled by common sense.

Giving our children and parents a choice is what matters most. Being forced to take a class founded on the general premise of blind pursuit of self-interest seems counter to Christian or other religious thought. Self-interest is defined as "consideration of advantages for yourself in making a decision, usually without worrying about its effect on others." As an example, when purchasing a car, a price is agreed to, plus tax, title, and license. The final paper work has sales tax and inventory tax. It is to the dealer's advantage to pass the inventory tax on to the buyer, even though the tax was levied on the dealership. Is the dealer greedy, lying, cheating, stealing, or pursuing self-interest? Many uninformed consumers pay the tax without realizing they have over-paid.

At a minimum, students and parents should be allowed to substitute Financial Literacy in place of Economics as a graduation requirement.

The State Determines your Knowledge

In the state of Texas, the legislature determines what the schools will teach and what classes your student must take to receive a diploma. These rules are explained in "The Texas Education Code." In summary, a student must take economics, with an emphasis on the free enterprise system and its benefits.

For a parent who doesn't know what is taught in the course, it is useful to examine either the TEKS from the Texas Education Agency or the AP College Board. A visit to the AP College Board website reveals an ad for the class.

What makes this course interesting?

1. Become familiar with the cost-benefit analysis that is the "economic way of thinking"

2. Understand smaller segments of the economy, including consumers and producers, their interaction in output and resource markets, and the impact of government

3. Learn to use graphs, charts, and data to analyze, describe, and explain economic concepts

This all sounds great to a parent that hasn't read this book or doesn't have the time to assess the details. Here is a quick comment on each of the three reasons promoting the course:

1. Cost-Benefit—"Economic Way of Thinking" The course does not teach cost benefit, but instead, teaches opportunity costs. Chapter 6 explained how opportunity cost hides profits. If a student truly adopts the "economic way of thinking", they will never find a job, as no business in the real world uses opportunity cost to determine profits. There is a reason why the Economics Department is not part of the business school.

2. The impact of government is predominantly described as a negative factor for the economy. The books portray regulation as bad:

   a. "... government rules to control the price, sale, or production decisions of a firm."[125]

   This sounds more like what happens in a centrally planned communist economy. No effort is made to provide a full description of the types of regulation that markets need to operate in a fair and safe manner. Consider the west Texas farmers near midland Texas that are paying over $8000 a month for electricity. This is not due to a "market failure" but due to regulation failure. The high rates are due to monopoly control of transmission lines. Common sense regulation must exist in certain markets. The book fails to explain other

   ---

125 Paul Samuelson, Economics, McGraw Hill, 2005, page 342

regulations such as margin requirements when trading stock or regulations that specify loan qualifications.

There is no mention of the moral hazard faced by banks lending debt to unqualified borrowers and then selling the debt on Wall Street as AAA rated investment. Moral hazard is briefly mentioned by Mankiw:

"The moral hazard problem is the temptation of imperfectly monitored workers to shirk their responsibilities."[126]

Government regulations are required to curb financial failures due to moral hazard.

3. Learn to use graphs and charts. . . . Chapter 5 provided a vivid description showing that economists have no idea how to use graphs charts and data, unless they are trying to deceive someone. Anyone trained in these methods becomes ignorant about how to properly use mathematical analysis.

Further reading of the Texas education code brings one to section 26, which defines the rights of parents in determining what their students must study. Bottom line, a parent can object to a portion of a class, but cannot prevent their child from taking an entire semester class. Imagine a graduation requirement that states the student must learn how to break a horse. If the state decides everyone must know how to break a horse, then so be

---

126 Gregory Mankiw, Principles of Economics, Sixth Edition, South-Western Cengage, 2012, Page 468

it. There is little to no option for a parent/student to avoid the instruction.

In Texas, until the State changes the education code, students and parents have no choice to avoid the economics class if they want to receive a diploma. This is probably true for most other states. The three bodies likely to influence graduation requirements include the state legislature, the state board of education and the education agency.

Taking Steps

In September 2017, I met with my state legislator, the state board of education, and a nonprofit organization, Jumpstart. The message delivered was the same for all three groups.

Our school system can improve tremendously with one simple change.

Problem Statement—

1. High school students are often disengaged in the education process by the junior or senior year, due to lack of relevance in the curriculum.

2. The high school economics class teaches outdated and irrelevant concepts that are not used to support any standard business practice.

3. The economics class is required for graduation, perhaps for traditional reasons.

4. The economics class requires a full semester.

5. Adding another course as a graduation require- ment would be difficult to accommodate, given the existing requirements.

The problems can be addressed by teaching a more relevant course, Financial Literacy, instead of Economics. Relevancy is improved without adding pressure on students and schools to support an additional graduation requirement.

In addition to changing the graduation requirements, all state universities should no longer accept College Board test scores for AP Economics classes. The material is out of date and will not improve the performance of students going to our Universities. AP economics teaches false mathematical concepts, lowering our children's ability to properly analyze various business situations.

Benefits/Justification:

1. Students learn material that is extremely relevant. Ask any student or parent to pick between Economics and Financial Literacy and they will select Financial Literacy every time. The only reason they do not make that choice today, is the graduation requirement and the lure of AP credit.

2. The risks of repetition of the 2008 financial collapse are related to a consumer's lack of understanding of high risk mortgages. Educating the public reduces the risk of financial failure for the entire country.

3. Students learn about starting their own small business. This represents an opportunity to boost our economy.

4. Students learn about the different ways to save for the future, increasing the health of our financial system.

A bill for Financial Literacy is a bill for the economy and the people of Texas.

Support the Change

A website, www.thetruthabouteconomics.com, will host supporting form letters that can be used to petition change from the various institutions involved. Sample letters will be found for the following organizations:

1. State Legislator—form letter that follows the "Message for Legislator" noted above.

2. University President—form letter asking your Alma Mater to stop accepting AP test credit on any economics class.

3. Local School District—A form letter to petition the replacement of economics with financial literacy. Each state is different. It may be possible for one to accomplish the goal without legislation. The availability of the class will vary by state. Some states require financial literacy to be taught upon request, even though it is not a graduation requirement.

4. Other documents and notices that support the goal will be on the site as well.

Perhaps the most important thing I learned is it doesn't matter how we arrived at this predicament. It could be the liberals, the conservatives, the Republicans, the Democrats, the Academics or Wall Street, who really knows? It doesn't really matter. What matters is we make a change.

I hope this book gives you the knowledge and motivation to help your kids and our future citizens learn what they

need to know about economics. A final quote from Robert
Heilbroner:

> "What lies behind the veil of economics?
>
> Our deep-lying, perhaps unanalyzable notions concern-
> ing human nature, history, and the like, and the various
> disguises by which we come to terms, especially in cap-
> italist society, with the primary but hidden sources of
> social orchestration—domination and acquiescence on
> the one hand, affect and sociality on the other."[127]

---

127 Robert Heilbroner, Behind the Veil of Economics, Penguin Books,
    1988 page 185

Acknowledgements

FIRST I MUST thank my wife, who patiently listened over and over and over as the thoughts for this book coalesced into a meaningful stream of words. It seemed I was a kid, with a new package of Play-Doh, and all I could do was talk about the great animal shapes forming in the other room. Thanks Sandy . . .

Next to thank is my circle of poker and golfing buddies. They were the early volunteers that read the first versions of the manuscript. Randy, Tom, Steve, Don and Joe provided excellent feedback, constantly encouraging me to keep it simple. Special thanks to Joe, who provided notes, comments, and excellent discussion along with good wine.

My fellow teacher, Angie, graciously took the time to read an early version of the manuscript. Her encouragement and feedback was a fresh tail wind as I wrapped up the final edits.

I was fortunate to have two of my students willing to take an early plunge. Jennifer and Nolan accepted the task and gave the book an early read. Their enthusiasm for the truth was fuel for my fire. I hope all future students find the merit and energy experienced by Nolan and Jennifer.

There were several professional economists that were kind enough to read a random email from me, and reply to an odd question here and there. They probably were not aware that their brief reply was like a stroke of a paddle moving me down river. The following provided motivation with the smallest bit of encouragement: Alain Samson from London School of Economics, Luigi Pasinetti from University Cattolica, Brian Martin from U.O.W. Australia, Jim Stanford from McMaster University, Philip Mirowski from University Notre Dame, Rod Hill from University New Brunswick, Jim Nolt from NYU, and John Pullen from UNE Australia.. Extensive encouragement was provided by James Galbraith from University of Texas. James wisely identified the most important facets of this story, our students, their education, and our future.

Most importantly, given my lack of appreciation for well placed commas, or any comma for that matter, I could not have made it without my editor, Petrena Wilbur. She demonstrated the patience of a great teacher, wading through the various drafts, calmly fixing commas and removing my frequent tendency to shout out my raw emotions on this topic. Thanks Petrena!!!

Bibliography

Chapter 1:

1. Joseph A. Schumpeter, "Science and Ideology", The American Economic Review, March 1949

Chapter 2

1. Gregory Mankiw, *Principles of Economics,* 6th edition, South-Western Cengage Learning, 2012

2. Joseph A. Schumpeter, *History of Economic Analysis,* Routledge, 1954

3. Piero Sraffa, "The Laws of Returns under Competitive Conditions". The Economic Journal, Blackwell, December 1926

4. Jacob Viner, "Cost Curves and Supply Curves", American Economic Association—Reading in Price Theory, Allen and Unwin, 1953

5. Allyn A. Young, "Increasing Returns and Economic Progress", The Economic Journal, December, 1928

6. Thomas Cate Editor, *An Encyclopedia of Keynesian Economics,* 2nd Edition, Edward Elgar, 2013

7. Steven Keen, *Debunking Economics,* Zed Books, 2011

Chapter 3

1. An interview with Robert Coase, 9/17/97 https://www.coase.org/coaseinterview.htm

2. George Stigler, *Theory of Price*, Macmillan, 1966

3. Philip Kotler, *Principles of Marketing*, Prentice Hall 2013

4. Peter Fader, "Marketing vs. Economics: Gymnastics or High-Wire Act?", Forbes June 15th 2012

5. Henry Schultz, "The Chicago Tradition in Economics Volume 5", Routledge 2002,

6. David Teira Serrano, "A Positivist Tradition in Early Demand Theory", http://www2.uned.es/personal/dteira/docs/positivisttradition.pdf

7. E. J. Working, "What do statistical demand curves show?", Quarterly Journal of Economics, Oxford University Press, February 1927 volume 41 issue 2

8. Henry Schultz, "The Chicago Tradition in Economics Volume 5", Routledge 2002

9. H. L. Moore, "Economic Cycles: Their Law and Cause", Macmillan, 1914

10. Michael Lewis, *The Undoing Project*, 2017, W. W. Norton Company

Chapter 4

1. Robert L. Heilbroner, *The Worldly Philosophers*, 7th edition, Simon and Shuster, 1995

2. Adam Smith, *Wealth of Nations*, Metilibri, digital edition, 2007